Overcoming Abuse: Child Sexual Abuse Prevention and Protection

A Guide for Parents Caregivers and Helpers

Reina Davison

WESTBOW
PRESS*
A DIVISION OF THOMAS NELSON
& ZONDERVAN

This book is a work of non-fiction. Unless otherwise noted, the author and the publisher make no explicit guarantees as to the accuracy of the information contained in this book and in some cases, names of people and places have been altered to protect their privacy.
The information, ideas, and suggestions in this book are not intended as a substitute for professional advice. Before following any suggestions contained in this book, you should consult your personal physician or mental health professional. Neither the author nor the publisher shall be liable or responsible for any loss or damage allegedly arising as a consequence of your use or application of any information or suggestions in this book.

WestBow Press books may be ordered through booksellers or by contacting:

WestBow Press
A Division of Thomas Nelson & Zondervan
1663 Liberty Drive
Bloomington, IN 47403
www.westbowpress.com
1 (866) 928-1240

Because of the dynamic nature of the Internet, any web addresses or links contained in this book may have changed since publication and may no longer be valid. The views expressed in this work are solely those of the author and do not necessarily reflect the views of the publisher, and the publisher hereby disclaims any responsibility for them.

Art Credit: Victoria Aleice

Scripture taken from the New King James Version®. Copyright © 1982 by Thomas Nelson. Used by permission. All rights reserved.

ISBN: 978-1-9736-8020-8 (sc)
ISBN: 978-1-9736-8021-5 (e)

Library of Congress Control Number: 2019919610

Print information available on the last page.

WestBow Press rev. date: 12/26/2019

RELEASE OF LIABILITY

This book has been written with the intent of providing helpful information on child sexual abuse prevention and protection. The author highly recommends the reader avoid skimming this book, as skimming could result in misunderstanding of the content and message. If, as a reader, you find this work on the dynamics, consequences, and proposed solutions to child sexual abuse offensive, it may be that you are not the intended audience. This book was not written to be used as a diagnostic tool or to treat any child sexual abuse problems; consult a mental health or medical provider for diagnostic treatment. The author and publisher are not liable in responsibility for any mental, medical, or economic needs that require professional supervision, and they are not liable for any negative consequences or damages from any exercises, clinical recommendations, or theological suggestions to any person reading or following the information provided in this book. Resources and references are provided for useful purposes and are information that may change with time and do not constitute endorsement of any organization, website, or other sources.

The facts, statistics, details, and data are presented as informational content and not to be held as the author's or publisher's endorsement. The contents are not a warranty or guarantee or implied belief of the publisher's choice to allow any of the contents in this book. The readers certify and agree that if any difficulty is experienced by reading portions of this book whereby past trauma is triggered that they will seek support. The reader is responsible for his/her own free-will choice to read the book contents and for any actions as a result of reading this book. Neither the author nor the publisher shall be liable for any personal, or otherwise, social media comments/reviews, loss, or injury or special, incidental, or consequential damages resulting from a person's choice to read this book.

The work in this book has been presented solely as a guide and educational source. The author and publisher are not offering a cure-all method for child sexual abuse. Neither the author nor the publisher shall be held liable to any person or entity with respect to alleged libel or alleged invasion of privacy caused indirectly or directly by the information contained in this book. Any similarity to any reader's profile or circumstances is purely coincidental. Each child sexual abuse circumstance has various dynamics which determine the interventions/strategies that may or may not be recommended for the particular abuse situation. Any definitions of child sexual abuse or scenarios cited which constitute immoral acts are solely described for the purpose of explaining the level of trauma experienced and are written about for the purpose of education. Child sexual abuse is an ungodly act. Sexual abuse in modern society is no different than that which is cited in the Bible as the immorality of Sodom, Gomorrah, and Babylon, and that which is spoken of in Judges 19:25, Deuteronomy 22:25-26, Leviticus 18:6, 2 Samuel 13: 5-17, and Mark 7:21-22.

There are realities and truths which are the foundation of child sexual abuse and that are against God's moral principles. The author, assistants in publishing, and the publisher do not endorse explicit immoral acts outside of the biblical principles, which are consistent with Christian morality. Any discussions of godless behaviors are presented not to have blunt discussions on amoral acts, but to present the truth about sexual abuse and to offer prevention, possible solutions, a reconciliation with God's moral principles, as well as a relationship with Him. The author, those involved in the preparation or publishing of this book, and its publisher assume no responsibility for any reader who chooses to label this book's contents as impure, obscene, or unholy material. To deny parents or caregivers access to information on how to prevent and protect children from the trauma of child sexual abuse or to remove the truth about child sexual abuse invites satan and the abuser to maintain the problem (sin) of child sexual abuse in our society.

The author has researched data and sources which are believed to be reliable information that is in accordance with the professional code of ethics and current standards of practice at the time of publication. In the event of the possibility of human error or changes in the medical and mental health sciences, neither the author nor the editor and publisher, or any other parties who were involved in the process or publication of this book guarantees that the information contained in this work is complete and flawless in respect to accuracy and they are not responsible for accidental omissions, errors, or any outcomes which result from the use of the information in this book. Readers are encouraged to consult with Scripture, continue the research contained in this book, and to confirm with additional sources.

But Jesus said, "Let the little children come to Me, and do not forbid them; for of such is the kingdom of heaven."

Matthew 19:14

CONTENTS

FOREWORD

Almost no parent talks about sex with their children! I recently attended a large conference where the speaker asked how many in the audience had a meaningful talk about sex with their parents? One person raised her hand. The next question was how many of you discussed sex with your children? Again, one hand was raised.

The sad truth is today if we do not discuss sexual issues with our children they will be ill equipped to navigate life. The problem is, most parents have no idea what they should say to their children. So we say nothing or we have only a few cursory words with our child in a very awkward meeting that is awkward for you and awkward for your child.

If you don't have the discussion, your children will learn about sex from internet porn sites or from each other on social media. This means they will learn about sex in all the wrong places. The issue is no longer an option. A parent can no longer assume his or her child will know how to recognize and respond to sexual advances from family, friends, and strangers.

A child who is unaware that offers of candy, kind words, or hugs are often the first step a sexual offender will take, is vulnerable to sexual abuse. This includes the trauma of sexual abuse which affects every aspect of a child physically, psychologically, emotionally, and spiritually for the remainder of their life. The question is, if a predator reaches out to your child, will he or she know how to respond? She will not know how to respond if you have not previously talked to your child. But, you may ask, how do I talk with my child about this issue?

The book in your hands will provide the information you need to address the issue of Child Sexual Abuse (CSA), prevention and protection. It is a guide for parents, caregivers, and helpers. The author, Reina Davison, has also written a companion book for preschool to elementary age children entitled, *My Body Belongs to God and Me*.

Overcoming Abuse: Child Sexual Abuse Prevention and Protection is divided into three parts: Part I, Educating self, child, and others about Child Sexual Abuse (CSA); Part II, Becoming aware of CSA and Implementing Safety; Part III, Overcoming Child Sexual Abuse.

The information in the forty one subheadings of this book will answer virtually every question you may have on child sexual abuse. Questions such as: how do you recognize a sexual offender? What is the prevalence of child sexual abuse? What is the impact of sexual abuse on a child? What should you share with your child now and at each age as he or she matures? What is a grandparent's role? What if I learn my child has been sexually assaulted?

The author, Reina Davison, has written her book through the lens of a loving God who loves every child. Davison is well-prepared to discuss the child sexual abuse issue. She studied Marriage and Family Therapy at the Karl Menninger School of Psychiatry and Mental Health Sciences, and is a marriage and family therapist. She also completed her Master of Clinical Social Work at the University of Kansas and a post-graduate program on Trauma and Abuse at the University of Texas. Davison has taught sociology, marriage and family, and cultural anthropology as adjunct faculty. She has worked with a multitude of populations including child day care, the military, prison, agencies on aging, in-patient and out-patient care in city, veteran's, private hospitals and private practice.

Finally, the book covers every area of child sexual abuse including healing from child sexual abuse, and there is also a resource with a long list of organizations that can provide information, help and advice -- organizations such as the National Advocacy Center, Childhelp USA, and the National Center for Missing & Exploited Children.

I encourage every parent with children, every grandparent, and all who teach or serve children to read this book and be empowered to share, teach and train the children in their care how to protect themselves from sexual abuse. It is our responsibility to ensure their safety so they are able to live a healthy joy-filled life, uncomplicated by the experience of sexual abuse.

Train up your child in the way he should go and one day your child will thank you!

John K. Graham, M.D., D.Min., MSc., President and CEO,
Institute for Spirituality and Health at the Texas Medical Center, Houston

ACKNOWLEDGMENTS

All praise and thanksgiving to the Creator of all things...the Creator of this book...God. It is God's Holy Spirit Who implanted the idea of this book and its ministry in my heart. Immeasurable gratitude goes to all whom I spoke with, shared with, and prayed with. A lot of you who prayed with me continued to pray for the publication of this ministry. Sometimes even strangers whom I met while conducting research or in day to day life united with me on this journey—which then further developed this book. Thank you to each of you for your support through the details of the publishing process and for joining forces with me on this mission to assist parents and those in the helping professions in protecting children.

Victoria Aleice, thank you for allowing God to use your gift of art in developing the cover for this book. Your ability to envision with me what the Lord had placed in my heart for the book cover along with what He placed in your spirit created the images depicted in this book. Thank you for becoming my ally in this ministry to help the abused and for taking me along with you through a divine color-filled adventure!

Mary Ellis Rice, you were and always will be the first proofreader and editor to each of my books in the *Overcoming Abuse* book series. You poured yourself over the manuscripts from the very beginning leaving me confident that you were not only skilled as a professor of writing but genuinely interested in being a part of this much needed service for the abused. Thank you for helping propel this work!

Jessica R. Everson, thank you for your editorial services which made a statement about your professionalism and supernatural powers of skill and time-management! Your work ethic will always be appreciated as a part of your care over this project.

Amy Mize, you have been an orchestrated appointment. Saying *thank you* cannot express the length of the extra miles you have gone with impromptu notice to assist with your photography skills. In spite of your various ministries inside and outside of home; you are always ready to give from the blessings of your talents. I am certain our Lord has looked down upon you and said, "Well done, good and faithful servant."

Thank you to all who have labored in the preparation and completion of this book at WestBow Press and to Bob DeGroff. Bob, thank you for your sincere, kind, and helpful attitude towards authors and all of those around you!

A deep thanks to all of you who invested *time* reading the manuscripts right before publication. *Thank you* for providing your valuable feedback for reviews.

Dr. Graham thank you for your generous servant's heart! In addition to your already overflowing responsibilities you willingly accepted the calling of reading two manuscripts from the *Overcoming Abuse* series and wrote a Foreword. Thank you for your God-giving spirit towards this ministration.

I am grateful for the blessing of my family of origin and to my immediate family who has prayed for my books to develop and for those books to affect lives for the better. Thank you to you that I love and am proud to call family. To my sisters-in-Christ to whom I have already disclosed, that I have declared you as family, including Mom Frazer; thank you for your encouragement of my writing, your prayers are intangible and I am grateful to report that they have been answered through the publishing of the message in this work...to *all* in this acknowledgment...this book is dedicated to you!

NOTE ON SELECTED TERMINOLOGY

For the purpose of readability and in an effort to select multiple universal terms, I have elected to use the words *child sexual abuser*, *spouse*, *abuse*, *perpetrator*, and *victim*. As a term, *abuse* can involve all forms and levels of victim and family sexual abuse. This book is not intended to be offensively sexist when the male gender is referred to as the abuser/spouse and the female gender is referred to in some pages as the victim. My true motive and intention for this book is that it becomes a manual on Child Sexual Abuse (CSA) for the child's parent/caregiver, helper, and any person that is interested in helping with the traumatic consequences of Child Sexual Abuse.

The labels of *sexual abuser*, *sex offender*, *child sex offender*, sexual *perpetrator*, *and sexual predator* are all used synonymously because they are the words used by professionals and researchers to describe a child sexual abuse offender. Whether it's pedophilia, hebephilia, or ephebophilia (attracted to pre-pubescent, pubescent, or post-pubescent children), the label or title of the sex offender is not significant because all titles represent all sexual immoral touch/assault of children and an impropriety of sexual conduct both in God's eyes and in the federal and state statutes under the United States law. It does not matter what label is given to the molester by the government, academia, society, the church, medical profession, law enforcement, or the judicial system; he is still guilty of committing a crime against a minor—child sexual abuse.

To maintain a clear and simple discussion throughout the book, I at times refer to the husband or wife as the *spouse*. When referring to the child *sex offender*, in some pages I have selected the term *perpetrator*, not because every perpetrator who has problems with controlling behaviors is a child sexual abuser, but because it is a word that applies to any person who has consistent, ongoing problems with manipulation, power, and control and has sexual thoughts of children and acts out those thoughts.

On most pages, I have elected to use the term *he* to refer to the child and the child sexual abuser. The masculine pronoun *he* is used for the sake of uniformity and word simplicity (applies to either male or female offenders or victims). This is not about denigrating men—it is the *characteristics* of child sexual offenders and the child victims of CSA that I am addressing, not their manhood. There are female sexual offenders. However, the term *he* is used because it describes the majority of the research done on child sexual abuse in which manipulation, power, and control are misused by male sexual offenders.

When writing about the child that is abused, I use the term *victim*, not because I view that child as a helpless dupe, but because it is a term that applies to any child suffering from act(s) of sexual abuse which have led him to have CSA trauma. In order to incorporate every potential medical professional, therapist, counselor or lay person (that may have an opportunity to work with CSA), I have selected the term *helper* as opposed to using the title of each profession or assistant.

The name *God*, His proper names, and pronouns referring to God are capitalized out of reverence to Him. Since capitalization is like italicization, it's a method that suggests "importance" and emphasis; I have elected not to extol satan's name, thus his name is not capitalized. Because God the Father, God the Son, and God the Holy Spirit are One in the same Trinity, I am referring to the three of them simultaneously when I'm speaking of our heavenly Father, since they are each equal as one God (1 John 5:7, John 10:30, Matthew 3:16-17, 28:19, 2 Corinthians 13:14). All scriptural quotations are from The Holy Bible, New King James Version. The same scriptural references may be quoted in parts of this book in order to expand on the verse, use it in a different context, or facilitate comprehension through a different example.

When referring to the *soul*, I am referring to the emotional and moral sense of identity. When speaking of the immaterial being, which is the nerve center for feelings and sentiments, I speak of the *heart*. I am not using the term soul in a theological form as the immortal part of the being. Conversely, when I refer to the *spirit*, I am then speaking about the mood or immortal and eternal soul, and spirit is not capitalized. The Spirit (Holy Spirit) is always capitalized.

The term *mindful* is used to describe the process of becoming aware of one's thinking as related to the mental technique of *mindfulness*—not as a religious ritual, but as conscious, mindful observations of one's thoughts, experiences, and behaviors.

Last but not least is the term *Overcomer*. Overcomer is capitalized as a proper noun and given importance because the word represents Jesus' work. It is also set apart from the other text for emphasis on the victims who through the power of Christ have overcome their abuse.

While working with victims of abuse, I have always elected to not use the term *survivor* when referring to any victim that has recovered from abuse. The reason is that I don't work with victims to help them to just exist; I want to encourage them to stop living a life of abuse—to permanently conquer and have victory over abuse! Being a survivor means to stay alive or to exist or live on. Synonyms for survive are *ride out*, *weather*, and *make it through*. But a victim doesn't just want to weather or ride out their abuse. They don't want to just make it through their trauma—they want a fixed line of defense.

When I set goals with victims or when I refer to those that have recovered from their abuse, I have always used the term "Overcomer." To overcome means to defeat or conquer. It's about being victorious over something. Synonyms for overcome are *stop* and *triumph*. The Greek word for *overcomer* literally translated means "victor." The verb (action) forms and noun (person) forms for *overcome* are "to conquer" (conqueror), "to have victory" (victor), and "to defeat" (defeater). The definition of *overcome* and to be an "Overcomer" is more fitting to the desire of every victim of abuse—and ought to be the desire of every society. One cannot say "survivor" while saying "victory." One cannot say "victory" while saying "survivor." One can only say "victory" while saying "Overcomer."

Moreover, in addition to definitions of an overcomer are the biblical definitions, which are also more fitting to the quest of a victim who seeks tranquility and a permanent resolution to an abusive past, present, and future. The Bible equips us with examples of how we are to live our lives. It instructs us on how to rise above our circumstances in order to live victoriously as Overcomers. A person does not have to be a victim of abuse to become an Overcomer. Followers of Christ are called various names, including *believers*, *little children*, *Christians*, and *Overcomers*!

HOW TO BEST USE THIS BOOK

Behold, children are a heritage from the Lord, the fruit of the womb is a reward . . . Happy is the man who has his quiver full of them.
Psalm 127:3-5

Dear Parent, Grandparent, Caregiver, or Helper:

You have been rewarded with the gift of a child! Some of you have been rewarded in plurality! However, with this gift, as with any, comes responsibility—to take good care of it. With this blessing, you have been called to train up your child in the way he should go so that when he is old he will not depart from it (Proverbs 22:6). What an honor!

But what *is* the way he should go? It's certainly not the way he *wants* to go, because all children and adults were born as sinners. And it is definitely not the way the world would want him to go, because that's satan's way (Ephesians 2:1-3). Then the way he should go is the way of righteousness, as is stated in God's Word. "Train up" is not a suggestion. It is a commandment for parents to raise their children from birth until they're grown with consistent instruction from God's Word (in spite of world's advice on guiding children).

Training your child is not a happenstance; it is a calculated effort to teach your child wisdom and healthy choices for his life. This training, which includes teaching your child about Child Sexual Abuse (CSA), must be done sooner rather than later. The bonus in that proverb, though, is the promise to the parent that when your child is old, he will continue to follow it.

But there is a caveat in child training. The training will most likely not be successful if the parent does not provide a consistent example of the righteous behavior being taught (in this case, respect for one's own body and body safety). A parent must live out what he expects from the child. The child must observe and experience body safety while growing up if he is to claim ownership of his body and command respect for it. What the parent teaches the child must be role-modeled and enforced repeatedly—training by example. Training also involves open communication, allowing the child to use his mind, to speak up, and to listen to you.

Yes indeed, your duty as a parent is to *intentionally* parent, just like God does with each of us. Our heavenly Father, as evidenced in the Bible, is an intentional parent. Those of us who have a personal relationship with Him experience His divine discipline as we go about our lives, following His callings and commandments. He speaks the truth to us in love through His Word (the Bible). God's Word instructs parents not to withhold speaking truth in love into their child's life. Speaking the truth in love is loving discipline. Discipline is a parent's responsibility, and speaking the truth in love teaches your child responsibility.

Parents should be mindful of the reality that children's deoxyribonucleic acid (DNA) does not contain responsibility. Responsible behavior must be taught and learned. Your child must be able to feel your strength through your teaching, training, and management of tough subjects. And he must observe your Overcomer approach to the problem of CSA. This approach must include time invested in helping them overcome (defeat) CSA, and instilling wisdom within them and their descendants. In doing so, your child will know that you expect defeat of CSA and nothing less. And by their fruit you will know that your efforts to train them up have been blessed!

The research clearly indicates that the leading challenge to overcome if CSA is to be prevented and children protected from victimization is the deficiency and absence of awareness regarding the dynamics and prevalence of child sexual abuse. To protect a child from CSA, parents, caregivers, helpers, and children must be trained. Training your child on CSA means instructing him on the difference between proper and improper body touch. It means protecting him from unsafe body touch.

You have been specially selected, assigned, called, and equipped to teach your child about CSA and body safety. I say equipped, because if you have already researched CSA or have picked up this book as a part of your research, then you're equipped! God *always* equips those whom He calls to a responsibility. And it is your parental responsibility to pass on that equipped awareness of CSA to your child at age-appropriate levels.

I have written this book to assist you in your endeavor. In addition, I've created a book for preschool to elementary age children entitled, *My Body Belongs to God and Me*, which you can use as a guide to help your child become aware and skilled on body safety. The children's book is meant to be read to younger children in more than one sitting, so that their shorter attention spans can internalize the concepts as a process. Naturally, as children age, the book will need to be re-read periodically until they mature into a full comprehension of God's role, a healthy adult's role, and their own self-protection plan to overcome CSA.

Sexual abuse is a challenging topic for most parents to bring into discussion, especially with their children. But, as unpleasant as the subject may be, sexual abuse is an essential conversation for all parents and caregivers to have with their children, because sexual abuse is a serious, heart-rending, everyday problem in our world that affects both male and female children. Also disheartening is the fact that the abuser is usually an older child or adult already known to the child, typically an older authority figure the child loves and trusts. Generally the abuser uses emotional force and manipulation, not physical coercion, to engage the child in sexual activity.

There are a lot of rude-awakening facts about CSA, but the fact that a child may or may not show any abnormal outward symptoms of child sexual abuse should set off a siren that ought to motivate every parent/caregiver to learn more about CSA and compel them into that must-have conversation with their child. If you're thinking, "This doesn't happen in my family," or "Not to families like ours," consider thinking again. The prevalence of child sexual abuse is real, and it is easy for those of us caught up in the fast-paced daily rat race filled with other responsibilities to miss the CSA data.

But there's still a way to catch up on the facts. One way to gauge the prevalence of CSA in your neighborhood, community, city, state, and nation is to ask yourself if you have ever known or heard of someone who has been the victim (or perpetrator) of sexual abuse. Chances are, the answer is yes, and probably more than once.

Sometimes when I travel and eat out, I ask my server this question: "I will be blessing my meal and praying for others. May I pray for you as well?" It's never a surprise when someone quietly discloses a need for prayer on CSA. That is how common this type of abuse is. Most of us have heard of someone sexually abusing someone or someone being sexually abused. It's just that, for the most part, the child sexual abuser and the victim go unreported to the authorities.

If you haven't heard the most recent child sexual abuse facts or need an update, here are a few facts to bring to memory a reminder of the importance of teaching children body safety. Let's begin with a crash course on the basic facts of child sexual abuse:

- The child is generally acquainted with the abuser, who may be a family member, friend, clergy member, teacher, tutor, coach, babysitter, or other authority figure.

- Child sexual abuse usually happens to a victim more than once. It can go undetected for months or years.

- Sexual abuse includes, but is not limited to, sexual behavior with a child through activities involving body or genital contact as well as non-body contact events, such as exploiting the child by showing him pornographic images or taking nude images of the child.

- Children with obedient, shy, compliant, respectful personalities are more likely to become victims of CSA.

- Children with a history of upscale authoritarian homes or who are from dysfunctional families are more susceptible to sexual abuse due to their affection deprivation, strict authoritarian upbringing, or lack of boundaries.

- Children who have been sexually victimized will either display none or some behavioral symptoms. The child may keep the sexual abuse a secret. Or, a child sexual abuse victim may withdraw from the usual things they used to enjoy, detach from family or friends, experience academic difficulties, sadness and anxiety, or become aggressive and engage in self-defeating and injuring behaviors.

How does a busy parent who works and who perhaps has more than one child and a household to tend prepare for such an important conversation with their child? By becoming well-informed about the dynamics of child sexual abuse and learning the skills to prevent and protect their child from sexual abuse.

There is a complete section in Part I on educating and training your child on CSA. However, keeping in mind that parents/caregivers/helpers are extremely busy or may be undergoing a CSA crisis with need for a quick read, summarized lists of strategies for teaching and training the self and child have been provided with subheadings throughout this guidebook.

Some important reminders are purposely repeated in these lists because as God said figuratively speaking, we are a stiff-necked people (stubborn/not wanting to be led). This human stubbornness is evidenced by the Israelites who ignored Moses' instructions from God. Yes, we are known to be disobedient and for resisting God and the Holy Spirit's guidance, both in the Old Testament and in the New Testament (Exodus 32:9, Acts 7:51). Repetition comes in handy, especially if you are in a time crunch and need to decipher which list applies! Do not get overwhelmed with the crisis and the amount of research in this handbook; read what applies to your circumstances. You can always refer to the necessary sections and the various lists when you are able.

When should you begin to read to and have a discussion with your child about body safety? Just as soon as your child has an attention span to sit still and watch an entire episode of a child's television program. If a child can sit and watch cartoons, your child is old enough to listen to you share body safety skills.

There is a lot of information covered in this book because most parents and caregivers have questions which must be answered if they are to approach their children on this subject matter with confidence. Once a parent has done the recommended steps, it is safe to say that they have taken responsibility to teach and train the child in present and future prevention and body protection.

God bless and provide for your every need in taking care of your gift—your child. Again, God always provides the means to support what He has asked of us. Pray for the courage, the words, and the strength to have that very necessary CSA training with your child.

What if your child has already been abused? There are strategies in this book for that as well. Remember, a child that has been empowered through your teachings on CSA will not only benefit himself, but he will also pass it onward to the next generation (your grandchildren).

Serving Him Along with You, Shoulder to Shoulder,

Reina Davison

PART I
EDUCATING SELF, CHILD, AND OTHERS
ABOUT CHILD SEXUAL ABUSE

For from within, out of the heart of men, proceed evil thoughts, adulteries, fornications, murders, thefts, covetousness, wickedness, deceit, lewdness, an evil eye, blasphemy, pride, foolishness. All these evil things come from within and defile a man.

Mark 7: 21-23

Child Sexual Abuse Defined

Child sexual abuse (CSA) takes place when an adult solicits and engages in sexual activity with a child. *Grooming* is also child sexual abuse. Grooming is the initial stage, when the sexual abuser befriends the child to develop an emotional attachment and reduce the child's inhibitions with the intention of sexually abusing him.

Although child sexual abuse is a crime in the United States (U.S.), across all fifty states there's a lack of acknowledgment and knowledge about this crime. Child sexual abuse is defined as inappropriately exposing or subjecting a child to sexual touching, behaviors, and activities. The abuse includes all types of sexual bodily contact with the hands or other parts of the body. It includes the use of objects for sexual stimulation. Sexual abuse incorporates inappropriate solicitation in person or online, sexual enticement, exhibitionism, and the use of sexually explicit materials. It also may include exploiting the child for pornographic purposes, making a child available for pornography, human trafficking, asking a child to engage sexually with another adult or child, photographing a child in sexually provocative poses, or asking the child to pose nude. Additionally, non-contact behaviors such as making sexual remarks to the child, indecent physical exposure, exposing the child to adult sexual activity by using technology, and voyeurism (watching the child undress or use the restroom, usually without the child's awareness) are all acts of sexual abuse.

Prevalence of Child Sexual Abuse

The statistics on the prevalence of the sexual abuse of children are alarming. But even more alarming is that the majority of sexual abuse cases of children under twelve years of age go unreported. There are more cases than we have on record, but no police reports to tabulate the true numbers. Hanson, Resnick, Saunders, and Kilpatrick's 1999 study concluded that more than 85 percent of adults who were abused as children say they never reported the abuse to authorities.

Yes, child sexual abuse is happening in our neighborhoods, our churches, and everywhere around us. However, the research reports that most of us are too busy or unwilling to pay attention to this devastating trauma because of a preference to remain in denial or because we don't want to get involved.

The 2010 Child Maltreatment Report, a research study done by the U.S. Department of Health and Human Services Children's Bureau, reported that 9.2 percent of child maltreatment victims were sexually assaulted. Studies of adults that were sexually abused as children reveal that one in three girls and one in seven boys have a history of having been sexually molested before the age of eighteen. About half of sexually abused children are sexually abused by adolescents or other minors (who often have a history of being sexually abused themselves).

The 2003 National Institute of Justice report revealed that three out of four adolescents who have been sexually assaulted were victimized by someone they knew well. David Finkelhor, director of the Crimes Against Children Research Center, found in his 2004 study that in 90 percent of child sexual abuse cases, the child knew and trusted the person who sexually abused them. Unless treated, sexual abuse trauma leaves a lifelong spiritual, emotional, and physical impact on the health of the abused.

Nine out of ten children know their sexual perpetrator. This means that while most media reports of sexual crime involve abusers who are strangers to their victim, we shouldn't underestimate the potential numbers of predators who have an established relationship with the abused. While sexual assault by strangers does exist and is a serious problem, it is not as prevalent as sexual abuse by persons already known to the child.

The National Center for Victims of Crime's child sexual abuse studies include a 1986 study which found that 63 percent of women who had been sexually abused by a family member also reported an attempted rape or rape after the age of fourteen. Other studies in 2000, 2002, and 2005 all concluded similar results. The studies found that a child who has experienced attempted rape or a rape during adolescent years is 13.7 times more likely to re-experience attempted rape or rape in the first year of college. And both males and females who have been sexually abused are more vulnerable to human trafficking or self-employed prostitution.

The average age for prostitution in the U.S. is thirteen to fourteen years young. The National Runaway Safeline's research states that within forty-eight hours of being on the street, one in three adolescents will be lured into prostitution. There's a stereotype that children who are exploited in human trafficking are all kidnapped by strangers or terrorists who hold them captive and prostitute them against their will. The statistics show, however, that runaway children are at a higher risk for being trafficked into the sex industry. The sex offenders in human trafficking have the same traits and dynamics as all child sexual abusers do—manipulating the child via promises of favors/gifts/money, feigned romance/attraction, lies and deceit, and threats of hurting him or others if he tells/runs away.

Some sex offenders are at first kind and loving to the victim, but then drug, beat, and force them into prostitution. Some children are exploited from home via the internet, and they continue to live at home and attend activities or school while being trafficked. Over 57 percent of girls who engaged in prostitution say they were sexually abused by a person outside their family. The sex trafficker usually targets children that come from dysfunctional families with minimal supervision.

Child sexual abuse is the same around the world. It can happen to children from any educational level, cultural or racial group, religious or non-religious affiliation, rural or urban society, and across all socioeconomic stratums. There's a stereotype that sex offenders are uneducated people; however, the research has shown that there are a high number of adult sex offenders who are college graduates and even have postgraduate degrees. A sexual predator can be an impeccable, prominent citizen in a community, and is more often than not indistinguishable from the rest of society. The only characteristic identical among all CSA perpetrators is that their minds lust for sexual engagement with children, and that they act out those lustful thoughts by sexually abusing a child.

The other commonality is that all sexual perpetrators whether they're within a circle of friends, clergy, or family, they are selfish and have no empathy or regard for variation in their own or their victim's ethnicity, race, social class, creed, disabilities, or sexual orientation. They don't sexually abuse children because they're mentally ill or because they have an "addiction." They are child sexual offenders who, in addition, may have a mental disorder or addiction. Mental illnesses and addictions don't cause the sexual abuse of children. The abuser's focus and sexual preference is children—that is all.

In 2004, Finkelhor's research estimated that more than 300,000 children are sexually abused every year. Other studies by Finkelhor on CSA found that the most vulnerable age group is between the ages of seven and thirteen, and that one in five girls and one in twenty boys become victims of CSA. In self-reporting studies, 20 percent of adult females and 5-10 percent of adult males recall being sexually abused/assaulted.

There's another population that preys on children and that is other children. Almost 40 percent of child sexual abusers are older or more emotionally, mentally, or physically advanced children. The 2010 University of New Hampshire Crimes Against Children Research Center findings indicate that seven out of eight juvenile offenders are at least twelve years of age, and 93 percent are male. These child perpetrators are of age to know and recognize sexual boundaries and amoral behavior. However, their stature overpowers the younger and smaller child so that the child cooperates, and the perpetrator capitalizes on being more experienced and knowledgeable about sexual behavior. Some minors that are sex offenders engage in bullying the child into submitting to sexual behaviors/favors. Some child perpetrators have been victims themselves or have observed abuse through pornography or in their homes. CSA becomes for them a form of deviance.

The statistics for child sexual abuse are a real eye opener, but the numbers leave out cases that go unreported. Our communities in the United States verbally confirm that it is our nation's duty to develop programs that support the optimum health of children, including their safety, coupled with the support of financial resources to prevent their domestic neglect and abuse. However, there must be a system put into place that goes beyond verbal agendas, policies and procedures, mission statements, and catchy slogans, such as those that cry out that our children are our nation's next impressionable generation. Creating more shelters, psychiatric units, and foster homes for abused children is not the answer; doing so only increases the expectancy that more children will need these facilities and that sexual abuse trauma is an accepted and expected way of life.

Our society will always have CSA because there is darkness (sin) in our world; but to increase domiciles for sexually abused children is to encourage the perpetrator to continue abusing. How about training our society on how to stop the perpetrator before he strikes? The foundation of children's programs must be an unyielding concern for the human rights of children as targets of spiritual, emotional, physical, and sexual abuse.

There is an insufficient approach to educating the entire population of the U.S. on basic body safety rights of children. The ignorance is there because only a limited number of people in the helping professions, some parents/caregivers, and those developing children's programs are trained in CSA prevention and protection. The U.S. continues to operate without full knowledge of the pervasive, long-lasting effects of child sexual abuse trauma. It is our society's obligation to humanity to not just talk about child development or implementing programs, but to take *action* to protect children from and prevent sexual abuse.

Raising child sexual abuse awareness is one key that will present the message to the United States of America that we are a people who will say "No!" to child sexual abuse. This is not just a parental and caregiver duty, but *everybody's* responsibility to children.

It is only in recent decades that the U.S. has uncovered the prevalence of child sexual abuse, and efforts are being made to acknowledge the existence of CSA and the long-standing detrimental effects on children. Americans go about their daily routines not cognizant of this problem because they are either uninformed, misinformed, believe myths or stereotypes about CSA, or are confused about the dynamics and how they're dealt out. Being ill-informed about CSA leads to parents/caregivers and children being unable to protect their family and future generations from CSA.

The secret of CSA must be revealed—not only the truth about its daily occurrence but also the severe traumatic damage that it does to children. Public education media needs to include the CSA message that this is a problem for and responsibility of all U.S. citizens. The transmission of this message to our society should be bound by an objective to put a halt to any tolerance for CSA.

Do you recall the classic tattle-teller, who catches his sibling or friend breaking a rule and taunts in a sing-song voice, "Na-na na-na boo-boo! I'm telling!"? America needs to decide to take full action against CSA by adopting that same attitude of "I'm telling!"

Be better! Be better at telling! A profoundly clear, factual public education message with doable proposed solutions ought to be disseminated not only into homes but also to the policymakers who can support breaking the silence so that more productive actions can be taken. By educating our nation, we can become a united, ignited force in creating a society that's safer for our children to live in.

The last couple of decades have demonstrated some progress in civil authorities and lawmakers working together to manage convicted sex offenders by publicizing their residences and locations. The U.S. has enacted the community notification law, which authorizes the public to have access to information about the registered sex offenders. These sex offender registration laws are also in place for law enforcement agents to use as a tool in protecting citizens and providing justice. Some counties, cities, and states actually notify their citizens through law enforcement officers when convicted sex offenders are residing in the vicinity.

Some communities have town meetings whereby law enforcement gives notice and education when a sex offender has moved into the area and explains what to do to protect children. These strategies are useful safety alerts and they do promote some CSA awareness, but keep in mind that it is only the already convicted perpetrators who are on these lists. Without further commitment to CSA awareness, recognition, prevention, and protection by parents, caregivers, and other responsible adults, much of the burden is left with the child. A child should not be parentified in this way! The commitment must be implemented by adults in communities *before* children are sexually encountered.

Yes, all adults must step up to educate themselves on the sexual abuser profile and the dynamics and trauma of CSA. It is a collaborative effort between healthy adults sharing information and resources to prevent CSA in their neighborhoods. And while establishing an increased awareness of CSA, we should encourage our community members to go beyond their neighborhoods and contact lawmakers to initiate improved systems on CSA awareness, prevention, protection, and actions toward reformed laws nationwide. There must be a nationwide consensus in which each person, without exception, appeals for change and takes action for the improvement and establishment of CSA prevention and protection programs and justice for the victims in both court systems.

Child Sexual Abuser Profile

Child sexual abuse is perpetrated by juveniles as well as adults. Forty percent of reported sexual assaults against children ages six and under are attributable to juvenile abusers, as are thirty-nine percent of reported sexual assaults against children ages 6 through 11.[1] Adolescent boys make up approximately 23 percent of sexual offenders.[2] Research findings indicate that from 40 to 80 percent of juvenile sex offenders have themselves been victims of sexual abuse.[3] Only a fraction of those who commit sexual assault are apprehended and convicted for their crimes. According to Center for Sex Offender Management, only 33.9 percent of sexual assaults against persons 12 years or older were reported to law enforcement.[4]

Most research shows the sex offender profile is fourteen to nineteen years of age when they begin to abuse children. Some characteristics that are within the profile of sex offenders are their typical disregard of social rules and personal space or the sexuality limits and boundaries of others. Child sexual offenders have been observed spending the majority of their free time with children and have minimum contact with adults. Some sex offenders have been known to ask their spouse to simulate a child or dress child-like during sexual relations. More often than not, they have a special child whom they favor as their victim and intermittently exchange the child for a new one. They maintain this pattern with children by threatening to hurt the child's family, friends, or pet if the child tells of the abuse. Some sex offenders keep the child silent by offering special rewards in return for submission.

Sexual offenders, whether of an introverted or extroverted personality, are aggressively vocal in using profanity to intimidate and threaten with vulgar name calling. The sex offender doesn't hesitate to use adult sexual language to address the child and discusses his sexual activities with them without reservation. Sometimes, if the sex offender doesn't get his way (or even if he does), he disparages the child's body parts. This can become a learned behavior leading up to the child's distorted view of the human body, engaging in vulgar language, finding humor in sexual jokes; and later as a grown up doing the same. The majority of sex offenders also use the internet to view child pornography. Child sex offenders often seem unclear as to the amoral inappropriateness of their sexual fantasies. In general, they don't appear to know the difference between appropriate and inappropriate affection with children.

Most sex offenders can maintain a life of secrecy regarding their online activity or sexual abuse of children for a prolonged period of time; however, this is not always the case. Some reach a point where their sexual inappropriateness with children gets in the way of important responsibilities. When a sex offender is discovered and confronted about his sexual abuse, he refuses to take responsibility and prefers to deny his offense. He downplays the damage he has caused and blames others or his circumstances, despite the obvious evidence and trauma suffered by the child. Because of this denial, families have a greater responsibility to take care of their children, not just within their own family system but in the community as well. If sex offenders won't take responsibility for their inappropriate actions, the responsibility falls on law enforcement, the medical and helping professions, parents, caregivers, family, friends, and society.

In my book *Overcoming Abuse: Embracing Peace Volume I,* I speak about setting up a prenuptial agreement that sets limits to your tolerance for abuse of any type to protect yourself and your future children from abuse. It is quite all right to ask your fiancé during your premarital counseling session if there has been any type of abuse in their family. You don't want to find out after you're married that there is a background of abuse. If there has been sexual abuse, for example, consider the fact that you will have to police your children that much more closely at family functions when the sex offender and/or his enablers are present. This should be a red flag for you before you marry into this family.

There may be family members who ignore the truth about the presence of a sex offender (and those who enable it) in the family by allowing the offender to attend family functions. This permissiveness not only re-victimizes his family members, but it also endorses his inappropriate offenses. This is not to imply that you should condemn the sex offender—that accountability and judgment is God's. Your place is to forgive him, but also to put boundaries all around you and your child when in his presence.

Some people assume that forgiveness includes staying connected to the perpetrator (of any type of abuse), but that is not the healthy solution. The resolve with a sex offender or any other abuser is to forgive and to have no contact whatsoever, so as not to enable his abuse. Staying in contact endorses his abuse of your child and others.

God is a Holy God of love, forgiveness, and kindness. If you have a personal relationship and are connected to God, He will transfer His holiness, love, and kindness to you, and you will achieve a higher, bountiful moral plane, which will resist the devil's temptation to ignore immorality. Instead of hatred toward the sex offender or inappropriate mingling with him, ask God to stand in the gap with you, to fill your heart with His all-embracing love, which removes grudges, bitterness, and vengeful thoughts of hate. God's holy life offers a quality of life to overcome CSA because His holy life within you is indestructible against the devil's CSA darkness.

The godliest and kindest act you can do for a sex offender is to refer him to treatment with a specialized sex offender counselor or to a sex offender program. They can call or email The Association for the Treatment of Sexual Abusers (ATSA) where they can obtain a referral to a local treatment professional or a program for sex offenders (ATSA phone number: 503-643-1023; email: atsa@atsa.com; website: www.atsa.com).

Most child sexual abusers who undergo treatment don't stop abusing children, because if they did, they would have to surrender their need for power and control and develop a sexual attraction to an adult who would not allow them to engage in child pornography or other characteristics of an offender. This is why the judicial system is able to require by court order that sexual predators register as sex offenders for life. The inmates with whom my colleagues and I have worked were all different types of child sex offenders, but the pattern of high rates of repeat offenses and recidivism was the same. What was interesting to prison guards we've spoken with was how often CSA offenders would return, knowing well that they were the most mistreated, bullied, beat up, and name called by fellow prisoners.

If you are thinking about closing this book right now because you can't even begin to imagine asking a suspected or convicted sex offender not to attend your family functions, I welcome you to do the research into the prevention and protection methods for child sexual abuse and to find out what the treatment approaches are for sex offenders nationwide and overseas. No contact—not even allowing a sex offender to look at your child, because offenders have sexual thoughts about children no matter the environment—prevents abuse and protects your child from the risk of sexual trauma.

All children vary as to the level of trauma they are susceptible to. Some will experience neurological damage even from non-touch abuse because the memory of the discomfort and exploitation remains intact, affecting their brain processing and psychosocial development. If you're still debating as to why a sex offender cannot be allowed around the children in your family, pretend for the moment that you are a child. If your parent/caregiver, relative, or friend knew that there was a sex offender in your family yet did nothing about his presence, would you feel nurtured, safe, and protected? The best prevention and protection for a child is to address the CSA problem with the offender and to let your child know that, because you love him, you are always going to be available to help him protect his body. The best help for the sex offender is to set boundaries around your child, other children, and to let him know that your child and family have a zero tolerance for child sexual abuse.

It is highly important to be a responsible parent/caregiver in teaching your child body safety. It is not just important to protect your child from the sexual offender in order to protect them from the offense itself, but also because children whose body boundaries have been violated by an adult suffer from severe lack of trust of all authority figures, including parents and caregivers. If your child is sexually abused by an adult, his perspective on trusting adult figures to appropriately nurture and keep him safe is different than that of a child who has never been violated. And if an adult does not protect their child from a known sex offender, it affects his relationship with that adult and other adults.

A child may not immediately reveal his feelings of anger or distrust over not being protected, but eventually his thoughts and feelings will be reflected in his behavior toward the neglectful adult and others. Some children do not show their disappointment, hurt, or anger toward the parent or other adults who did not protect them, but the feelings stay with them. Adults who were sexually abused as children look back on the adult(s) who did not protect them with a lack of respect, and they become aware of the detached bonding in their relationship.

Do not allow any sister- or brother-in-Christ to judge your decision to remove yourself or your children from the presence of a family child sex offender. Do not let them tell you that you have an unforgiving spirit and a lack of understanding about redemption. This is not biblical truth. It is not God's will for anyone to subject themselves or their children to child sex offenders—it is God's position to deal with sex offenders, who are accountable to Him for their sin. Your only duty is to prevent the abuse and protect God's children from immoral behavior (sin). This is not a time to worry about not being liked or approved of by family members or being shunned for standing up against child sexual abuse.

Don't worry about the comments from family members who respond to your decision to set boundaries with the sex offender. Ignore comments such as, "Oh, so you think you're better than us," or "I guess you're holier than thou now, and our family is not good enough." Those comments or thoughts about your decision to not enable the sex offender are based on the ignorance of those family members about the true nature of CSA, or because of low self-esteem. It could be that they have been abused themselves and may have never done anything about it or are taking your decision as a personal rejection of their past, themselves, or the family. Regardless of the reason, this is not a time to focus on the objections of family members.

The healthy, functional attitude is to speak up and create boundaries of prevention and protection within the family system by setting limits with the offender. It is the full responsibility of all adults that know about the family sex offender to protect by agreeing to set up a Body Safety Family Plan to prevent unwanted inappropriate child body contact. Children should be taught body safety, regardless of having a family perpetrator, but it is not solely the children's responsibility to keep their bodies safe.

When you find out that there's a sexual predator in your family after you're already married into the family, the best strategy is to speak up and prevent and protect by *not* attending family activities when the sex offender is present. This teaches your children body safety as you role model that it's okay to say no to child sexual abuse and abusers.

There may even be friends who disagree when you share your family's body safety plan. That's when it's time to part ways with those who don't support your decisions, even though it may be hurtful. And if they reject you, God is still on your side. He is for you and not against you (Romans 8:31). God's warning and command has always been to not associate in friendship and relationships with those who waver on the borderline of God's principles. God has warned and commanded us not to keep company with unholy people because we become those with whom we associate. We're to build wise friendships with others who hold mutual godly interests and to love others into finding God's will for their life. This is what Paul wrote about regarding not keeping company with and separating ourselves from immoral believers (1 Corinthians 5:9-13).

Our life is not our own. Our true help comes from our Lord, Who made the heavens and the earth. When your friends and family decline to help you design a Body Safety Family Plan or to coordinate CSA resources or to report CSA and they leave you, you're still covered under His precious blood (love) as He directs your paths! A righteous (godly) attitude toward you when you share your Body Safety Family Plan should be an attitude of understanding and support, if not excitement, assistance, and an "I'm on it!" Or, one might agree with you in prayer and offer to pray for your Body Safety Family Plan. That one prayer from that one friend may do more than you can even imagine. You've probably heard it said that one prayer from Moses did what two million grumblers couldn't do!

Why Do Child Sexual Abusers Abuse?

Child sexual abuse, as with all types of abuse, is about power and control. Most sexual offenders declare that they feel more in charge when sexually engaging with a child than they do in their relationships with adults. There are various reasons (excuses) that sexual predators use to validate their abuse of children. Some abusers blame unemployment, break-ups or divorce, or alcohol, drug, or mental health challenges. Some perpetrators openly state that they are more sexually attracted to children than adults.

Some sexual offenders have a history of neglect and/or abuse and violence. However, having such history is just that—a history. Although coming from a dysfunctional family background or having mental health or addiction challenges increases the risk of becoming a sexual offender, the majority of victims with a history of abuse live a lifespan without ever sexually abusing other people. Of the convicted sex offenders, about 80 percent have themselves been exposed to abuse or were sexually abused themselves, but nowhere near this percent of abused people act out and repeat their sexual abuse.

The idea of why a person would choose to sexually abuse a child may appear incomprehensible, but with a better education on the psychiatric dynamics that motivate them, we can better understand the nature of CSA and the need for prevention and protection.

There is more than one type of sex offender. For instance, most people think that all predators are pedophiles (attracted to prepubescent children), but the only common thread with *all* child sexual offenders is that they're in pursuit of a relationship they can control. Children are innocent and easier to entice, to convince to keep a secret, and to manipulate, compared with adults.

Some examples of common types and subtypes of sex offenders which sometimes overlap are as follows:

- The *fixated* offender is generally an immature adult who began his interest in sexual activity with children during his adolescence. There is an intense preoccupation with children and an absent interest in age-appropriate relationships. The majority of these offenders target male victims and become repeat sex offenders.

- The *predatory* offender premeditates their CSA. They have sexual fantasies about children, engage in viewing child pornography, observe their victims for a time to selectively choose their target, then groom the child into a sexual relationship. Predatory offenders choose the perfect setting to abuse: in the home, by dating a woman with children, in churches with young families, in jobs that keep them in contact with children.

- The *opportunist* offender has sexual thoughts about children and may engage in child pornography viewing, but does not necessarily premeditate acting out their fantasies. This offender may work in a place that gives him access to children or a relationship with a woman that has children, and discovers that he is tempted to abuse. Being in a leadership or authority position over children gives him an opportunity to engage in CSA. Opportunist offenders use this same authority within the family system because of their position of being known, loved, and trusted. An opportunistic offender may or may not groom his victim. The opportunist offender may be friendly or physically forceful; he may not have self-control and may act impulsively on his power-centered, self-entitled authority.

- The *regressed* offender maintains age-appropriate relationships and may engage in sexual activity with a child as an inappropriate means of coping with stressful circumstances. This offender falls in the subtype of being more of an impulsive, situational, or opportunist offender in contrast to the predatory and fixated offenders who plan out their activities and groom their victims. Regressed offenders know their victims (usually females) to whom they have convenient access during their stressful times within their family or friends circle.

Not all sex offenders fit into a neat category, type, or subtype. However, at the end of the day, all child sexual abusers rely on an opportunity to have access to the child, alone.

- Some child sex offenders are introverted loners with minimal adult social skills. They work at jobs that do not require a lot of contact with people, especially other adults. They have a low self-image and carry themselves in an awkward, child-like way, appearing odd or eccentric in their demeanor and/or attire.

- Other child sex offenders are extroverts. They do not isolate themselves, but instead make themselves visible as good citizens to eliminate any suspicion. Both the introverted and extroverted sex offender abuse because children appear less intimidating than adult peers.

- Sex offenders typically have a sense of entitlement and a self-privileged attitude that leads them to believe that they deserve to have or do whatever they want without taking responsibility for their actions.

- They typically have a sense of accomplishment after deceitfully manipulating the child, the parent/caregiver, and others through the grooming stage.

- Sexually deviant behaviors excite the offender, including a variety of sexual behaviors and addictions.

- They typically have a negative view of their body image and low-self-esteem.

- They are typically unable to manage daily life stressors and are needy for unmet emotional affection. They use children to obtain sexual gratification and cope with life stressors.

- Most offenders deny their CSA, but if they admit it is wrong, it's temporary, until they're with another victim, then they again rationalize and minimize the severity of the harm and immorality of their act.

There is simply no moral reason, justification, or excuse for behaving sexually with a child. In today's world, adults as well as children have access to online sexual content in chat rooms and easy connection to child pornography, which does not deter sexual predators from acting on their urges. The internet has the capability of desensitizing children, adolescents, and adults from the perversion of child sexual interaction by making sexual relations with children appear as a standard or normal behavior. No matter what the internet normalizes, the only truth is that the trauma of CSA is severe and may become a lifetime experience for its victims. Consequently, it is important to teach CSA prevention and protection, because once a predator abuses the child, it will happen again and again if not intervened upon. The average child sex offender preys on twenty victims.

Sex offenders are known to have had a poor parent-child attachment growing up, then they pursue inappropriate affection to compensate for their lack of parental love and nurturing. Child sex offenders have minimum awkward relationships with adults but tend to relate well with children. If they are married, they report an unfulfilled relationship.

The child abuser longs for power and control over anyone, as he feels powerless otherwise. They're seldom caught sexually abusing the child, but they give themselves away to be suspected because they tend to break rules and press the limits. A child's parent must be able to recognize these signs and help demystify "the secret" the abuser wants the child to keep.

A sexual abuser, as with all abusers, is very adept at discombobulating what is truly going on between the child and himself. The child is confused, as can often be the parent or caregiver, by his questionable behaviors. The parent/caregiver is left to use mindful thinking and to trust their intuition to resolve the puzzle if the child has not told "the secret."

The following are some examples of inappropriate interaction between adults and children which cross boundaries and can alert a parent that there is a red flag:

- Prefers to set no limits/rules with the child

- Seeks the child's approval and friendship

- Insists that the child sit on his lap, or on a hug or kiss when greeting or saying goodbye

- Persistently seeks the child out to hold, carry, give piggy-back rides, or tickle/wrestle, even when the child has said no and is obviously uncomfortable

- Ignores or refuses the child's requests to set limits, even when the child does not want body contact

- Ignores the social, emotional, and physical boundaries voiced by the child, and makes others feel anxious or uncomfortable in his presence

- Has no filter or boundaries, and exposes the child to sexual references/interactions between adults made on television or has adult conversations with occasional sexual jokes in the child's presence

- Walks in on the child when he is using the restroom/shower

- Frequently offers to play with, bathe, change, or babysit the child for free

- Teases the child or makes fun of the child and encourages others to laugh at them when the child voices discomfort and attempts to report him and to set limits

- Has a preoccupation with emailing conversations or attachments (games, photos, and sexual sources), texting, or calling children or youth

- Maintains secret contact with children and adolescents, offering gifts/money, help with homework/tutoring, sharing alcohol/drugs

- Invites children/teens to his home or on outings alone

- Has no boundaries nor self-control. May approach a child even in the child's home, public setting, or place of worship

Child Sexual Abuser Grooming Behaviors

Do not assume that the sexual abuser will only groom the child in private. While that may be, most of the time the sexual offender develops his intimate relationship with the child within visual distance of family or other people. The abuser's ploy is to make people not suspicious of him. He plays on the minds of those who can't imagine that an offender would act out his inappropriate behaviors at a family gathering or public place. The scheme of the child sexual abuser is to create a false sense of trust with the family/other adults so that they and the child believe his behaviors are *not* inappropriate and that the child is safe.

The following is a list of some of the engagement or grooming behaviors of a child sexual abuser:

- Tells child he is special, the only one who understands him, and that he favors him over his spouse

- Attends child's sports or other public activities

- Treats child different than other children. Flatters child and offers romantic relationship

- Tells child to keep it a secret about the special time he spends with them or what happens between them

- Treats child like an adult while he behaves like a child

- Gives child select privileges while making the child feel obligated to comply with his requests

- Does not allow child to befriend peers or play like other children do

- Looks at and inspects the child's body and says it's to check on his body development

- Accidentally-on-purpose enters the child's room when he's undressed or walks into the restroom while the child is there

- Inquires or makes allegations regarding sexual activity between the child and peers

- Shares private information about the child's parent, his own mother, or spouse

- Consistently treats the child badly in front of others (as a cover up)

- Disrespects child's privacy, not knocking before entering room, not allowing doors to close in bedroom and bathroom

- Engages in physical contact, massaging and rubbing, wants to bathe child

- Talks to child about the child's body and clothing in a sexual way

- Accidentally-on-purpose brushes past child's private parts

- Accidentally-on-purpose touches child's private parts while wrestling, horse-playing, and places his body against child's

- Teaches human sexuality by showing child pornographic images, shows his body and asks for nude photos of child via phone, sends his nude photos to child's phone, and asks child to delete photos after viewing

- Asks child to give him back/leg rubs while on couch, asks for child to help wash his back while in bathtub

- Comes into child's bedroom for talks or while child is asleep, touches child

- Talks to child about his sexual experiences, tests child's reaction to affection/touching

- Offers child a special gift if child goes alone on an outing with him

- Walks around nude in the house when parent/caregiver is out or accidentally-on-purpose leaves his clothes unbuttoned/unzipped

- Rubs lotion/ointment on child for no known reason when parent/caregiver is not home

- Constantly wants to be alone with the child, makes excuses to go places with the child/for people to leave, spends more time with children than with adults

Stages of Child Sexual Abuse

Seeks to Gain Access

When a child sexual abuser doesn't have a "special" child or is limited in access via family and friends, often his target becomes a child who appears unsupervised and is not savvy about body safety, is withdrawn, not confident, or perhaps appears sad/troubled. The sex offender's immediate need is to meet the child and have access through gained trust and control. The offender watches closely and determines the level of attachment between the parent and child while looking for an opportunity for alone time with the child. Sometimes he appears to be a helpful neighbor offering a parent/caregiver relief from their childcare duties by playing/coaching, giving a ride/taking the child to an activity, or inviting the neighborhood children to a sleepover party.

Misuse of Power, Trust, and Authority

Not being suspected is the name of the game for a child sexual abuser. A sex offender will feign an adult romantic relationship, date, and even marry to cover up his sexual thoughts and interests. This allows him to gain access to children through the adult relationship.

Most accessible children have already observed that their parent/caregiver trusts the offender, so he capitalizes on that established trust. The offender's goal is to appear to care for the child's valued adult relationships as well as for the child. He showers the child with special privileges/favors/gifts to lure him into a connection. The child becomes torn and trapped between relying on the offender's trusted image and the feeling of powerlessness and fear of consequences if he tells on this authority figure.

Crosses Limits and Boundaries

An offender will spend long periods of time scheming his access to the child before grooming and abusing his victim. He has trial-run tests on limits and boundaries to evaluate the parent/caregiver and the child's response/reaction. When a child is uneducated about his body parts, appropriate and inappropriate body touch, and the importance of his bodily privacy, it's more likely that the offender will be able to make CSA appear as normal appropriate touch. This gives the offender an opportunity to break boundaries by pretending that he is teaching the child appropriate behavior because the child is innocent and does not know any different. He trusts the adult figure.

At this point, the offender has already identified his prospective victim by gaining access and trust and maneuvering the child's defenses. The pushing and crossing of limits and breaking boundaries are not just aimed at the child; they include manipulating the parent/caregiver, leaders, activity staff, and the community-at-large.

Controls and Silences

Child sexual abusers prefer long-term, lasting abusive relationships, so they work diligently to ascertain that the child will keep the abuse a secret. They use numerous approaches to make certain that the child does not tell. One manipulation tactic is to threaten to harm the child, his loved ones, or his pet. Another tactic is to induce guilt and shame, telling the child that he is bad and at fault and that his parent/caregiver will punish him. Sometimes the child's family is undergoing difficulties, and the child does not want to add to the burden with the secret. Some children fear not being believed.

Child sexual abusers are able to exploit and control their victim because of the power imbalance based on authority, stature and strength, age, and life experience. This creates a status that overpowers the child's ability to speak up, especially if the abuser has gained the child's trust. There are exceptions, though, when trust has been violated; then coercion, force, and fear keep the child silent.

The Reasons a Child Victim of Sexual Abuse Does Not Tell

Following are some of the reasons a child does not tell about the abuse:

- Blocks the trauma out of his mind consciously or unconsciously

- Has an absent parent/caregiver and no trusted adult to tell

- Is pre-verbal, does not have the vocabulary to tell, or is too young to understand what's happening

- Is confused between right and wrong or what the rules are because the abuser says it's just a game

- Feels he will disappoint parents and cause family problems

- Feels scared and ashamed

- Fears not being believed

- Fears being ridiculed by his parent/caregiver, assuming they will think he's bad

- Believes he is to blame

- Fears parent/caregiver consequences

- Fears parent/caregiver as he has previously disclosed and now it has happened again

- Fear of being rejected/shunned for disclosing within the family and community

- Becomes emotionally/physically bonded with and dependent on the sex offender

- Feels compassion for the sex offender and does not want to get him in trouble

- Feels sorry for the offender and wants to take care of him

- Fears the sex offender will follow through with threats to hurt him/family/those he cares about if he tells

The Child that is Most Vulnerable to CSA

Following is a list of the characteristics of those children who are most vulnerable to CSA:

- Fears saying no to adults

- Fears being reprimanded and punished

- Fears being judged and labeled as bad if he's not compliant

- Has a void of unmet needs

- Feels needy for love, nurturing, and affection

- Has some form of disability

- Has a parent/caregiver/family who is uneducated about body safety

- Lacks healthy parental age-appropriate education on the body and human sexuality

- Is accessible to the offender because he is loved and is trusted to be alone with the child

- Can communicate freely and secretly with the offender (computer/phone/etc.)

- Is subject to the offender's power and authority

The Child Sexual Abuse Victim Profile

Following is a profile of the typical victim of child sexual abuse:

- No social behavior problems, well-behaved at home, school, and church

- Obeys in-home and out-of-home rules

- Compliant with doing homework and performs average or well in school

- Respects authority figures

- Has been raised to be an obedient child

- Has been taught to respect adults and not to talk back

- Has been trained not to whine or complain

- Has been taught not to be a gossip or tattle-teller

- Has been told to be polite and not to insist on his way only

- Has been told not to be stingy and to share

The Consequences of Child Sexual Abuse

Child sexual abuse (CSA) can cause serious damage to a child. CSA oppresses, exploits, and denigrates a child, ultimately leading to impairment of their cognitive, social, emotional, and physical development. As indicated in earlier pages, the physical symptoms of child sexual abuse are not easily detected, as most abusers avoid physically hurting their victims so they can sustain the abuse over time. However, it is also common that a child may inadvertently show signs of over-the-top sexual behaviors, which should then automatically identify the child as a victim of abuse.

CSA can be mostly undetected. Few children will have diagnostic symptoms. If a child is sexually assaulted (raped), then the harm becomes more evident. The child may complain of severe headaches or stomachaches, and extragenital trauma may be visible with vaginal or rectal bleeding, swelling, discharge, itching, or genital pain. Some children experience impaired bowel movements with painful urination. Other children contract sexually transmitted diseases (STDs) or get pregnant via sexual abuse.

Some advanced warning signs from child sexual abuse include fearful anxiety, insomnia, eating disorders, volatile moods, regressing into infantile attitude and behavior, fear of adults, repressed anger, isolation, suicidal ideation/attempted suicide, juvenile delinquency and personality disorders. Behavioral and emotional consequences may include intrusive thoughts, nightmares, heightened startle response, poor concentration, and hyper-vigilance, and in some cases, the child may appear depressed, withdrawn, or lethargic. Children will commonly respond to their victimization with sexualized behaviors and/or age inappropriate knowledge of sexual activities.[5]

The consequences of child sexual abuse may include severe low self-esteem, despair and hopelessness, chronic helplessness, self-mutilation, self-neglect, body dysmorphia, gynecological disorders, physical inactivity, or they may become obese to deter sexual advances, suffer gender dysphoria, wear provocative or, conversely, overly conservative attire, or exhibit promiscuity.[6]

Other long-term consequences for victims of child sexual abuse include:

Increased likelihood of teen pregnancy: *In one study, men who were sexually abused at age 10 or younger were 80 percent more likely than non-abused men to later engage in sexual activity resulting in teen pregnancy.*[7]

Increased likelihood of homelessness: *A study of homeless women found that childhood maltreatment, including physical, verbal, and sexual abuse, was a "pervasive and devastating predictor of dysfunctional outcomes, including chronic homelessness.*[8]

Increased risk of drug and alcohol use: *Research indicates that both women and men who have experienced child sexual abuse have an increased risk of drug and alcohol abuse in their adult life.*[9]

Researchers have found that the most common mental health disorders in society are anxiety, eating disorders, ADD/ADHD, substance abuse, and depression. The statistics show that millions of people are diagnosed with these disorders in the United States and internationally. Taken as read, these are also the primary diagnoses for victims of sexual abuse trauma. Researchers who calculate data have taken note of the substantial unreported CSA (which victims disclose during studies) and the evidence from the population at large who have the identical diagnoses. They postulate that more studies must be done on the correlation between unreported CSA and the most common mental health diagnoses within populations at large.

Some victims experience post-traumatic stress disorder (PTSD) symptoms of fear and anxiety, reacting with terror toward people who may resemble or share the voice qualities or characteristics of their offender. Some never recover from the sexual abuse and grow to have severe social difficulties in interacting with others as well as in romantic relationships. Adult sexual functioning may be impaired. Children can undergo a traumatic sexualization experience which may affect their development of a healthy, appropriate sexuality.

Other victims of CSA remain angry at their being hurt by someone they loved and trusted. They have problems trusting any authority figures. Other victims of CSA remain angry because they depended on a parent/caregiver to take care of them and they failed. Victims can continue to feel helpless and hopeless, just like they did when the child sexual abusers repeatedly manipulated them, brainwashed them, disrespected their privacy, and coerced and forced them against their will.

A lot of child sexual abuse victims become biologically attached to their abuser through the secretion of the oxytocin hormone. Oxytocin is the hormone in the posterior lobe of the pituitary gland (at the base of the brain) and is sometimes called the "love" or "cuddle" hormone because it is released when people socially bond or have affectionate body contact, and it plays a role in the social interacting and bonding between a sex offender and the victim. Some studies show that oxytocin can even be released while playing with a pet. Oxytocin can also be secreted when a person thinks about a bad bonding memory. It can be released when a person feels discomfort or resistance to a person they see as outside their inner circle of friends/family. The secretion of the oxytocin hormone depends on the person's environment; it can be a cuddly or a suspicious feeling.

Some victims don't lose the guilt they feel over the CSA because they believe there's truth to the offender's allegation that they caused it. That they are the one who broke the parent's rules and ought to feel badly and ashamed. Child sexual abusers are good at *projective identification*, reversing all his negative thoughts or feelings about himself and projecting them onto the victim. This leaves the child feeling deeply deviant and stigmatized as "damaged goods" and responsible for the abuse.

The National Center for Victims of Crime cites that when a victim is repeatedly victimized by the same or other offenders, the history recycles, and research estimates the increased risk of being re-victimized is over 1000 percent. Re-victimization is one of the most traumatic outcomes of CSA because repeat victimization augments the symptoms of prior CSA.

One of the types of sexual abuse that produces traumatic lifelong effects if not treated through mental health care is incest. As with other forms of CSA, incest is not partial to any ethnic group, race, creed, or economic status. Incest can thrive in the most impoverished or prominent households; it can involve parents and all next of kin. Unless it's a distant relative, incest usually skips the grooming stage, since a loving relationship has already been established. Sibling abuse is one of the most under-reported forms of incest. There's limited data on the prevalence of this type of CSA, but when it is reported, it is usually an older sibling that victimized a younger sibling.

One of the reasons incest is so traumatic is because it destroys deep trust in the family. The trust is now violated and severed. The child's first experience with love and trust is experienced through the foundation of the family system; that foundation is destroyed through incest. Some parents/caregivers take CSA and the laws into their own hands by believing the myths and stereotypes about child sexual abuse and not reporting when it has occurred. The correct approach is to take responsibility and work with the facts and truth about CSA.

When a parent/caregiver has been sexually abused in childhood but believes that the family member offender would not repeat the abuse into the new generation or abuse children outside of the family because the offender is now disabled, older/elderly age, or because they stopped the abuse with them (remember predators usually exchange their children for other victims after a time), this belief puts the present and future generations at risk for CSA.

Adults who finally confront their childhood sexual abuser or disclose their CSA may be misunderstood, stereotyped, incriminated, blamed, or judged by those to whom they disclose. Often, this happens when people lose sight of the fact that the adult victim was once a child who was incapable of consenting to sexual relations.

Child kidnapping alerts or CSA news on the internet or television may cause victims of CSA to revisit their trauma and be re-victimized when they hear, read, or think about the case; this is especially true for victims that have never told anyone or whose case was never tried. These CSA victims have experienced a "silent crime," because they have not been able to come forward due to the multiple reasons victims don't tell, including being submissive to those others in the family or the community who silence them, insisting they not report the crime. In doing so, these complicit others enable the CSA crime and the sex offender to prevail.

The Child Sexual Abuser and the Judicial System

Is there any justice for a child who has suffered and has been traumatized by child sexual abuse?

A victim of child sexual abuse can seek justice either through the criminal or civil justice systems. The difference between the criminal justice system and the civil justice system is that the criminal system requires a burden of proof and conviction must have proof beyond a reasonable doubt. The criminal justice system is controlled by the state, and the victim's role is to be a witness for the prosecutor.

The criminal justice system initiates the process after the sexual abuse crime has been reported to law enforcement. If the child sexual abuser is arrested and charges are filed, he can be prosecuted for a crime against the state. Then, a guilty or not guilty verdict is determined.

In the civil justice system, the proof of liability is necessary through preponderance of evidence. Proof beyond a reasonable doubt is not necessary. The civil justice system allows the victim to direct the decisions in the case, whether to sue, accept a plea/settlement offer, or go to trial. The civil justice system does not determine the guilt of the sex offender. Instead, the determination is made on whether the sex offender or a third party is liable for the trauma sustained by the victim as a result of the CSA crime.

In some cases, the civil justice system may provide CSA victims with monetary resources to help them reestablish their life. CSA victims have a right to file civil lawsuits pursuing financial compensation from the sex offender and others involved in allowing the CSA criminal activity. In the civil justice court system, the victim of CSA must prove that there is a 51 percent or greater chance that the sex offender committed the charges. There is a possibility that the victim can file for justice in civil court, and the offender be found liable even after they've received a not guilty verdict in the criminal court system.

Criminal and civil lawsuits have statutes of limitations (SOL) in both court systems; each state varies on the time limits set by law for filing with either court. If a suit is filed past the expiration of the SOL, it is time-barred and cannot go to trial. In some CSA cases in which victims have repressed memories or have been unable to speak up because of fear for their life/loved one's life, the time for filing may be extended. Contact legal aid, the National Crime Victim Bar Association, or your attorney to obtain information about CSA SOL in your state.

The criminal justice court can order the sex offender to reimburse select expenses incurred by the victim as a result of the crime or monetary compensation for any mental/medical health professionals or family/caregivers who have provided care/services in managing his/her trauma. However, even when the criminal court orders restitution, it is not always collected. The lack of follow through and enforcement of collecting court-ordered fees and penalties together with the limits on what damages are ordered for restitution usually results in the victim receiving little to no restitution.

The state compensates victims for losses due to a crime committed against them from the state's crime victim compensation fund. The losses reimbursed include expenses such as lost wages and other out-of-pocket costs, medical/counseling bills, and funeral expenses. The reimbursement is reduced by any insurance payments or other sources of compensation for the results of the crime. All states have laws on the amounts that can be compensated for a victim of crime as well as other eligibility and restrictions.

Educating & Training Your Child on CSA

Training a child on prevention and protection from CSA is not rocket science. Parents/caregivers who shy away from addressing CSA teaching miss the mark, regardless of their reason. Whether because they don't feel comfortable handling the subject, feel ill-prepared, consider themselves too busy, too tired, are taking care of their own needs first, or have to search for more information, they miss the prime time when their child is ready, and this sets up the opportunity for an abuser to enter the arena. Ask yourself, "Is my being uncomfortable more important than my child's discomfort when an abuser approaches him with unsafe body touch?"

It is simple to address the problem of unsafe body contact with a child. If dogs can be trained to be in the military and taught how to detect danger, contraband, and explosives before they inflict harm, a child can certainly be trained not to be ignorant of CSA, and a body safety plan is one way to teach CSA and an effective solution to the problem. But when children are clueless about CSA, it causes personal and social dysfunction, which can lead to greater trauma consequences.

CSA consequences *are preventable* through ongoing parental/caregiver body safety training. That is what's tragic—that a truly preventable trauma is allowed to fester in family homes and all over the world when the most effective solutions are so simple and readily available. Studies show that, unfortunately, CSA comes in the door because of parental/caregiver permissiveness. Permissive parenting only leads to a home without boundaries and the escalation of a child's self-will ruling the home. Children require instruction and guidance on everyday life, including CSA. It is a parent's/caregiver's duty to go to war against CSA.

The consequences of CSA not only affect the victim and their family, they impact generations to come, which beget increased levels of CSA. CSA is on the increase, not because of the children, but because of the abusers and the systems that work with and enable CSA, including parental/caregiver systems. Sometimes the systems spend their time concerned with how training a child on CSA will negatively affect them. But the truth is, there are no negative results from being informed about CSA protection.

Every loving parent/caregiver should *carpe diem* (seize the day) and get to work to put a stop to CSA, beginning with their own child. As with all children, their minds were not created or prepared to receive or experience any form of disturbing sexual information. A child can experience secondary traumatic stress just by listening to a peer self-disclose CSA. Secondary traumatic stress is the emotional pressure which results from hearing or watching any trauma experiences of another firsthand. Secondary traumatic stress can be inflicted upon a child hearing about sexual abuse incidents, body/gender dysphoria, or any kind of sexual confession from peers. *Train your child to tell you if this happens to him.* And always thank and praise your child for seeking you out to tell you of any body safety concerns for him or others. Even for a CSA-trained child, it takes courage and candor to share these things with adults.

Child sexual abuse must be reported, not just because it's a criminal offense, but also because all children have a right to be protected. Adults are mandated reporters. If your child shares with you someone else's CSA experience, be sure to get as much identifying information about the peer and the disclosure so you can report it. Train your child to say, "I'm sorry to hear that happened to you (or, "I'm sorry you feel that way about your body," if that's the case), but *please* don't talk to me about this anymore. You need to talk to an adult about this. I can't help you, but an adult can." Teach your child to immediately but confidentially tell a trusted teacher or school counselor about the disclosure.

This provides safety follow-up for the peer and a therapeutic ventilation processing opportunity for your child (so the secondary traumatic stress does not sit in your child's mind, creating emotional duress symptoms). Your child will not feel helpless and powerless over the peer's sexual problem because they recover by taking action and having an adult *do* something about the problem. Thank your child for understanding that you must do the responsible act of reporting his peer or friend that's at risk for CSA. Your child needs your reassurance that reporting a CSA incident is the right step to take because CSA is against God's morals, the morals of society and against the law. Help your child comprehend that CSA is a crime that cannot go unreported, and that it is *everyone's* responsibility to keep children safe.

Create a body-safe home environment for your children. Create an Overcomer home. What is an Overcomer home? An Overcomer home is a home where parents/caregivers choose to live in peace and do not allow tribulations (troubles, including CSA) to be the ruler of the home. The living Christ is declared as the only ruler of the earth *and* of the home life of the child. Teach your child what Jesus said to us in John 16:33: *These things I have spoken to you, that in Me you may have peace. In the world you will have tribulation; but be of good cheer, I have overcome the world.* Let your child know without a shadow of a doubt that he lives in a home that has overcome (defeated) CSA, just like Christ overcame the cross!

An Overcomer is a peace-filled parent who pours out age-appropriate wisdom, which results in a peaceful, safe home life. There is never an excuse or reason to be defeated by CSA in an Overcomer home. Are you an Overcomer? How does a person know if they have the characteristics of an Overcomer? An Overcomer wants God's presence and will in theirs and their children's lives; nothing more, nothing less, and nothing else!

The Bible calls on parents to instruct their children on God's principles and to help them grow into God-honoring adults (Deuteronomy 6:4-9). However, some of the very characteristics which help them develop into "good children" are the same characteristics that fit the profile of sexual offender targets: obedient, authority-respecting, well-behaved, godly boys and girls. Some parents have come to me feeling disgraced when their compliant child has been taken advantage of by a perpetrator, feeling as if they failed the child and set him up to be victimized. Just like it is never the fault of the child for being approached by an abuser, it is never the parent's fault for raising a child to be polite to authority figures. It is always the fault of the perpetrator, because children are not spiritually, neurologically, emotionally, or physically mature to consent to sexual activity.

Neurological research has shown that the human brain does not fully develop until the age range of twenty-five to thirty. That is why some car rental companies will not lease a car to an adult younger than twenty-five. The prefrontal lobe of the brain, responsible for managing discernment/right from wrong, decision-making or judgment, anxiety, impulse and emotional control, and drawing insight from the consequences of choices made, is still developing.

A child is not able to use good judgment on what to do and how to protect himself from CSA without a parent/caregiver teaching him. There is a risk at this developmental stage that the child will use poor judgment. Sex offenders will invariably tell the child that he's at fault because he allowed the abuse to happen or chose to let it continue, or they will outright say that the child gave consent. The truth again is that a child is incapable of giving consent, and this excuse can never be used by an offender or others who blame children or adults for their CSA because a child, as well as a differently abled/impaired adult or elderly adult, do not have the capacity to make consenting decisions or choices.

There is truth in the fact that some children are more of a prey to sexual abusers than others, and one of those reasons includes children who are more vulnerable because of their compliant nature. However, a parent's warning and preventive training of a child against sexual abuse can eliminate the problem of a child submitting to body abuse by an authority figure. A parent can educate their child by alerting them to CSA without frightening the child away from all authority figures.

It's important to keep in mind that, along with teaching your child the difference between respectful and disrespectful behavior, CSA training cannot be left out. If you're not doing the teaching and you're not providing your child with accurate information about CSA and their body from God's perspective, if you're not providing the support they need, someone else will come along, prey upon their innocence and naiveté, and provide misinformation that will influence their respect for their and others' bodies. Needless to say, children are vulnerable and impressionable; their ability to discern what defines respectful healthy behaviors is influenced by those around them. You be the one that's around your child and in his sphere of influence in every aspect of his Spirit, Mind, and Body!

In the health profession, using a holistic approach to our wellbeing means aligning the body, mind, and spirit in that order. I believe in and am in favor of a holistic approach to medicine and mental health; however, I elect to align a person's wellbeing in the order of the Spirit, Mind, and Body. When I work with patients, the Spirit that I refer to is not the same as secular spirituality. Secular spirituality adheres to the person's spirit being one without a relationship with God, the inner peace that comes from the individual. Secular spirituality focuses on humanistic qualities without divine intervention. Secular spirituality relies totally on the person nurturing their own thoughts, emotions, and actions without the supernatural power of God.

The Spirit which I refer to and work with as a Christian therapist is the Holy Spirit, Who is capable of dwelling within each human being. A child can be raised to use discernment by being mindful of his Spirit, Mind, and Body as he goes about his life making decisions and choices.

> *Do you not know that you are the temple of God and that the Spirit of God dwells in you? If anyone defiles the temple of God, God will destroy him. For the temple of God is holy, which temple you are (1 Corinthians 3:16-17).*

Take time to teach your child how to use his Mind in the most productive and effective way when he makes choices. Explain to him that his Spirit plays a role in developing and shaping his Mind. Let him know that the Spirit Who dwells in him helps the Mind to always check situations and to explore whether he is using his thoughtless free will or his well-thinking wisdom which comes from God. Remind him that the decisions and choices he makes affect him first and then others, in both the present and future. Tell him that seeking God's help and His Will for his life—and for others' lives—is called *mindfulness*. Say to him that mindfulness means purposely paying attention to his present experiences, moment by moment as they happen, without reacting with *mindless* thoughts or actions (choices). Let him know that mindless thoughts or actions are the opposite of mindfulness, and are symptoms of brokenness in the Mind.

Regarding his Body, teach him it is to be balanced with the Spirit and Mind. Train him to know that aligning his Body with his Spirit and Mind brings about a healthy Body, because balancing one's Body means treating our Body with respect by taking good care of it. Tell him that respecting his Body means taking care of his Body when you are unable to be with him, like when he's at school, by eating nutritious food, washing his hands, and using Body safety rules. Let him know that when he respects his Body, he is also taking care of his Spirit, Who lives in him, and that caring for his Body honors God, Who created his Body.

The following list is not exhaustive, but it is a start on the parenting path to raising God-honoring children who are safe from the world of CSA:

- Teach your children the difference between right and wrong behavior; teach them God's principles of respect for our Spirit, Mind, and Body.

- The role of the parent is to teach children to behave properly, because choosing right from wrong brings honor (respect) to God. Teach your child the negative consequences when he chooses the wrong behaviors. However, make it clear that choosing good behavior is not to be done in order to avoid God's consequences.

- Teach your child to choose his righteous actions based on *mindful* thinking (right thinking) (Romans 12:12).

- Teach your child about God's infinite wisdom and that He only allows the natural, negative consequences of bad behavior to take place so that He can lovingly help us learn to make the right choices from our mistakes.

- Never spill your wrath over your child or shame him when he shows signs/symptoms of CSA as it may hurt his spirit and discourage any bonding (attachment) with you as a parent or deter disclosure of CSA for fear that he will be deeply scolded and in unforgivable trouble.

- There's a difference in training a child to be obedient to God as an authority and training obedience to humans in authority. To obey God in reverence and fear of God's consequences and knowing why it is important to submit to His Authority is different than submitting to *all* authority figures. A child raised to obey mankind out of fear of authority and punishment is different than a child who obeys God's authority based on believing in His unconditional love and wisdom, trusting Him to know what's right from wrong . . . the child accepts God's consequences in compliance because doing so honors God.

- A child needs to be taught to understand that God is the ultimate authority over humans and all His creation in the world. A child must learn from a parent to honor God and all He has called into authority and that not all who are older in age or are adults have authority over them. The child must be taught to recognize that His parents were ordained by God to train him as a "heritage" from Him (Psalm 127). A child must be made aware that caregivers, relatives, or church or school staff may serve as authority figures for a time or purpose, but they are always operating under the primary authority of God and the parents.

If a parent teaches their child the principles of God-honoring behavior without submitting to all human authority, will the child escape the prospect of facing child sexual abuse perpetrators? Not necessarily, because we still live in a sin-filled world. One way to know if preventive measures and protection from a sexually depraved world are taking place in your home is by using yet another checklist. Ask yourself the following:

- Do parent and child understand the organization and structure that God has set in place for honoring authority?

- Do parent and child recognize God's rules of order (including morality) in our world from home, to community, to government laws?

- Are parent and child united in following God's biblical authority?

- Is God's Word being followed as an authority above world standards?

- If there are two parents, are both parents presenting a united front on spiritual and all other guidelines?

- Is there any form of rebellion to God's authority or others' authority in the order of the home life?

- Does the parent model what is expected of the child or does a double standard exist?

Why are the aforementioned questions relevant to the connection between whether a parent will prevent and protect a child from CSA or enable it? Those questions are important in determining whether a child will become vulnerable to CSA or not because if the parent(s) and child are not bonded and the parent(s) are not operating from a consistent, united front and do not know nor understand God's supreme authority and His rules of order in the world, then a parent and child will not be able to identify or know how to manage a breakdown in God's authority or the structure of His world.

A child who understands divine authority and the authority of God's structural order will defend himself and answer to a perpetrator in the way his parents want him to. A child who comprehends divine, home, and government order will answer in a commanding voice, "I am not allowed to do that!" or "That's against the rules!" When a child is trained on CSA, it won't matter if the authority figure is persuasive or forceful with intimidation; the child will obey God's authority with the same spirit his parents do.

A child trained in God's authority and moral order will not easily be dissuaded from the prevention and protection skills he has learned. The child will see their parent as the primary authority and will communicate to the parent if a perpetrator attempts to get him to say or do things against his upbringing.

There's also something magnificent to be said about the extra edge that a parent's or a child's instinct/intuition has, which, for a Christian, is the power to sense a prompting from the Holy Spirit that something is not right about an interaction or a situation. It's undeniably urgent to follow those promptings because they empower discernment between right and wrong. As a parent, that prompting must not be ignored or denied because it is useful in distinguishing when something is not correct or is unsafe for them. In addition, teach your children to pay attention to and sense their Holy Spirit promptings and convictions. This will direct them that it's best to lean into and follow their spirit's instinct rather than repress the safety warnings within.

To be forewarned by the Holy Spirit/instinct means being equipped to cope with any signs of body safety danger encountered in the present and future. Unfortunately, there are a lot of people who disregard their Holy Spirit/instinct warnings, and then they are surprised and hurt by the consequences of their choice. Taking the Holy Spirit's prompting seriously enhances faith and trust in God's guidance. This conquers fear and provides the ability to take steps toward CSA prevention and protection, meeting the incident and any future incidents with conviction and confidence.

What if the perpetrator is a part of an organization that upholds God's principles and moral order, like the church? God's Word instructs that parents or other authority figures must appeal to the church as an authority in these situations in order for God's protective righteousness to prevail (Matthew18:15-35). The parent and child must learn to appeal to all of the proper authorities, such as Daniel did (Daniel 1:11-16). This is in addition to government laws that require reporting to civil authorities (the police/FBI, judicial system).

What if a Christian parent or caregiver is the perpetrator? First of all, it's unlikely that an obedient parent who has a genuine personal relationship with God and who truly understands God's supreme authority and moral order would sexually abuse a child. Nevertheless, the child must learn that parents and caretakers are not exempt from being reported, and the child must be taught to do as the apostles in the Bible taught when they said, *We ought to obey God rather than men* (Acts 5:29). A child who has been taught to obey God's guidance over man's will choose to please God and, in general, will be surrounded by others who love and obey God.

A child who is shown God's love and is taught that God commands obedience (1 Samuel 15:22) and that He blesses those who wholeheartedly obey Him (Psalm 1) will aspire to honor Him and Him alone. The child must be educated on clear boundaries for amoral behavior and coached not to blur those boundaries with foolish or sinful responses to what has already been deemed as unacceptable for body safety. Teaching the child about the healthy hierarchy and a proper channel of authority to follow when a perpetrator attempts to entice him is crucial for the child to learn to appeal for himself along with his parent.

If a case of CSA does involve a parent/caregiver as the perpetrator, the predominant tactic involves control and manipulation. The controlling parent teaches the child never to insist on his own way and to bow to all authority figures. If the child is not taught to tell whenever he experiences attempted CSA, it usually results in a misguided behavior because of a neglectful or controlling parent/caregiver. This is also a form of projective identification. The parent/caregiver projects a thought or belief about CSA onto the child. The adult's CSA projection pressures the child into feeling, thinking, and acting according to that projection. This allows the parent/caregiver control over the child in denying/distorting the CSA reality in order to maintain a good public parental/authority image.

When projective identification takes place, the child's behavior is influenced and altered, making the parent's projected belief about CSA true (The reverse of what the parent is telling the child he is doing wrong regarding CSA is true). Unfortunately, the child then only learns to be compliant out of fear for authority and ultimately turns out to be as controlling as the parent/caregiver who guided him. The opposite is true if the parent trains the child to be respectful and loving toward others (Luke 6:31) based on his love for God and others (Matthew 22:36-40). This child will emulate that love and respect for others and live his life confidently in obedience to God's ways and those of his loving parent and family.

When a parent teaches a child that his body belongs to God and himself (1 Corinthians 6:19-20), he is trained to resist a perpetrator who wants to lead him astray, even if that person is a parent or caregiver. The child is armed with the knowledge that God is there to protect him, as well as higher civil authorities from whom he can seek advocacy and resolution. The child must be instructed that God ordained church discipline and civil authority to form a government of discipline for the perpetrators and all moral sinners of this world.

There are several examples of sexual assault in the Bible; one of them is found in 2 Samuel 13:1-22. If your child is sexually assaulted, it's most important to console and reassure them that this can happen in a sinful world, but that he is not responsible for the perverted sin of a perpetrator who overpowered him. To overcome his trauma, the child, in addition to appealing to and receiving the assistance from civil authorities, must be connected with solid biblical counseling—someone who will come alongside him with the clinical support and counseling needed to deal with the fear, rage, shame, sadness, anxiety, and other symptoms that come from CSA. Biblical counseling is suggested because it can present to the parent and child the presence of a sovereign God of love and grace Who will engage in the healing process and bring His comfort to restore peace through His Holy Spirit. Together with a biblical counselor, a parent or caregiver can facilitate the formulation of solutions to the aftermath of child sexual assault.

It is an act of re-victimization to tell a child to keep an attempted sexual assault a family secret. This is not in the child's interest for healing. Keeping sexual abuse silenced is for the convenience of the perpetrator or the authority figures who are uncomfortable or fearful of how it would affect them if it is reported. Keeping sexual abuse or attempted abuse a secret is not a biblical command. Christ always has and always will speak up when anything is out of order from His commands. There are numerous examples of Christ's disapproval of unrighteous behavior, such as when he was disgruntled with the boundary breaking at the temple (Mark 11:15-19).

It is very okay for a victim of attempted sexual abuse or a sexually abused child and parent to feel angry and to appropriately confront the crime. A child who is indoctrinated to do what is right—to honor God first—will respond differently than a child who is fearful to tell for the convenience of the parent or family or caregiver. A child who is taught to always speak up, in good times and bad times, will indeed have a voice for what is right. This is a child that a perpetrator will not want to target!

What if your child, after being raised under godly counsel and being trained in CSA, chooses the opposite of how you trained him? At the close of day, God will judge you and your child separately. You and your child will be accountable to God individually for His main assignment or calling and purpose for your life. Frankly, the Bible says that our heavenly Father holds us most accountable to love Him above everyone and everything else in this world with all of our hearts and minds, to believe in Him, to trust Him with the life He gave us, to follow His commands, including loving others as ourselves, to be still and listen to and obey His commands, to not rely on our own understanding but instead to acknowledge Him and believe that, in spite of our circumstances (or path our child chooses), He will direct our paths into the abundant life He has promised us.

God's Plan for Our Bodies

Protecting a child from sexual abuse involves a parent becoming educated on God's purpose for creating our bodies, learning about God's healthy perspective on human sexuality, and teaching the child God's views and plan. God has absolutes about how we should do life—including the care of our hearts and bodies—and how we parent. The world may have its lifestyle, but it's not always in sync with God's plan for our Spirit, Mind, and Body. Most parents learn about their bodies and God's creation of human sexuality through their parents. But if that's not the case and the parent doesn't feel confident about teaching his/her child body safety and sexuality in God's way, then the parent needs to begin by searching God's Word to gain a biblical understanding. The following are a few scriptures to begin your study on God's plan for our bodies and human sexuality as He created it. You may use these to have your discussion on protecting your child from sexual abuse:

- **Genesis 1-2, Psalm 139:** God created the world so that we could live in it with Him. He created our bodies in our mother's womb. He said our body is very good, and it is a gift from Him. We are to take care of our body, and His plan is that we take good care of the world He gave us as well.

- **1 Corinthians 6:19-20:** Our body belongs to God, and each of us has ownership of it. Because we own our body, it is our personal responsibility to take care of it. It is a parent's responsibility to teach and train a child to behave responsibly with his body by eating healthy, resting, practicing hygiene, and maintaining moral and bodily purity. Another reason for taking special care of and respecting our body is because God's Word tells us that our body is the temple of the Holy Spirit (His Spirit lives in our hearts).

- **1 Corinthians 7:2-4:** A child can be given age-appropriate guidance about his sexuality and taught that his body was created by God for the purpose of sharing only with his spouse in marriage (Song of Solomon). The child can learn that it is not that sex is a sin or that it is bad, but that it was not created to be experienced by children or anyone outside of the context of a marriage between a husband and wife. A child must be versed early on that God expects purity before matrimony by way of abstinence (1 Thessalonians 4:3-8) and purity in marriage through fidelity (monogamy) (Hebrews 13:4).

- **Romans 12:9-13** A child needs a lot of nurturing and appropriate affection from their loved ones. A parent, family members, and caregivers should be the foundation of demonstrating love for one another. It is the healthy, nurturing bond of affection from the parent/caregiver and child relationship that is the best protection of a child against sexually immoral behaviors at all age levels.

To help with teaching a child age-appropriate body safety and to prevent sexual abuse, the children's book entitled *Overcoming Abuse: My Body Belongs to God and Me* can be ordered through www.overcomingabuse.info and other book sellers. The book teaches the child about His body, which God created, and how to decline touch they are uncomfortable with as well as how he and his parent or caregiver can enlist a safety plan to protect his body.

Teaching CSA Safety at Age-Appropriate Levels

To assist in describing the child development process and its dynamics, I have used the eight stages of psychosocial development coined by Erik Erikson, professor, clinician, and child psychoanalyst who is best known for his book *Childhood and Society* and his research contributions on child psychology. Erikson's concepts of child development take into consideration external factors, parents, and society. Erikson's participant observation research and clinical studies indicate that individuals must go through the eight psychosocial stages, not just during childhood, but over the course of their life.

Erikson found that successful mastery of each stage resulted in the acquisition of strengths and qualities—virtues. Erikson's studies concluded that there is a direct influence and connection between social interactions and relationships and the role they play in the growth and development of human beings. Erikson's research notes that when a psychosocial stage is not successfully mastered, it may later in life result in a return to the problems encountered in that stage. However, it is not required that a stage be mastered or a virtue acquired in order to move on to the next stage.

According to Erikson, the outcome of a psychosocial stage is not permanent; there's a possibility that the stage can be modified by future life experiences. This doesn't mean that the responsibility of the parent and child to work toward the mastering of each stage are removed, because it is not a guarantee that modification will take place later.

Some trauma victims' psychosocial growth is interrupted or stunted, and they don't complete all psychosocial stages. Others just choose not to modify. That is what is meant by the saying, "Some people die at twenty-five and aren't buried until seventy-five."

Erikson's eight stages of psychosocial development and virtues are as follows:

- Trust vs. Mistrust—*Hope*

- Autonomy vs. Shame—*Will*

- Initiative vs. Guilt—*Purpose*

- Industry vs. Inferiority—*Competence*

- Identity vs. Role Confusion—*Fidelity*

- Intimacy vs. Isolation—*Love*

- Generativity vs. Stagnation—*Care*

- Integrity vs. Despair—*Wisdom*

Since this book is written about children, I will only cover the first five stages which focus on the virtues of—Hope, Will, Purpose, Competence, and Fidelity. I have combined Erikson's Stage 2 the virtue of Will (Toddler/Early Childhood years—eighteen months to three years) with

Stage 3, the virtue of Purpose (Preschooler—three to five years). I combine these two because the CSA concepts apply identically to those two age groups.

Birth to Toddler – HOPE

The focus for the parent or caregiver at this stage is to nurture and keep the child safe. The child is constantly searching for the parent's visibility, eye contact, and healthy touch. The child will develop feelings of security and trust during this stage, and will be confidently optimistic (hope) about the people who care for him. During this stage, a child can either develop a bonded trust or feelings of insecurity, feelings of worthlessness, and a mistrust of the world around him.

Infants develop rapidly into toddlerhood, not just physically but also in self-regulating their brain and motor coordination skills. All of their skills, such as crawling, scooting, pulling themselves up, walking, and talking, are influenced by what they learn from adults. They're also learning how to meet their emotional needs and learning to trust, which influences their feelings of safety and security. This is a very vulnerable stage because adults are highly counted upon to teach and aid in the development of the child. An infant or toddler can either have a negative body and self-regulating development experience and lose trust in adults or be positively influenced neurologically and physically. He will learn if he's in a safe family and can trust interacting with others and the world around him.

During this stage, the foundation of *trust vs. mistrust* and *autonomy vs. shame* is developed. Protection can be demonstrated not just by the parent or caregiver, but also with the intentional development of a safe family culture where open communication is encouraged at all vocabulary levels. Children can be shown protective safety even when they're non-verbal because they can see and hear safe actions. Teach your infant or toddler body safety through you and your family and friends' influence. Respect for the body and body safety are being taught as they learn when to say yes and when to say no. Body safety must be incorporated into the teaching of household and societal rules.

Even if your child is only babbling or not talking fluently, you are still teaching him the names of his body parts. This is helpful if your child ever needs to name a body part that he's concerned about or if he has discomfort in an area or needs to make a disclosure. Pointing to the body part can be helpful, but being specific is best because it prevents a misidentification. Train your child that his body is wonderfully made and that he should be proud and not ashamed of the very special body he has.

Sex offenders often label body parts by making up names for them which they believe will be seen as fun in an attempt to make the child believe the sexual abuse is just a game. In reality, many of these labels make fun of or degrade their body parts. While this practice confuses the child, if he has been taught correctly, he can always fall back on the proper names and good messages.

Most infants are unaware of the differences between boy and girl genitals, but by toddlerhood they may notice siblings and ask questions. Whether they do or don't notice, it's important to continue to teach the proper names for their body parts, and between the ages of three and four they should be taught that boys and girls have different genitals. This is done to assist in teaching them about privacy.

During this stage, a child thrives on routine schedules and consistency in patterns. They can easily become anxious or upset if things are not kept at an even keel. Before age two, teach them that some body parts, like the genitals, are to always be covered by diapers, underwear, etc., unless they are using the bathroom or being cleaned. Explain that the genitals are private and are not to be shown to or touched by others. The child may not be fully verbal, but he can hear you say things like, "And now that you're squeaky clean, let's cover up your privates!" "The privates are yours. No one is to look at or touch your privates except when you need help dressing or cleaning yourself." "When you go to the doctor, you may not be covered up, but I'll be there the whole time." "Remember I told you your privates are private? That means you should have privacy when using the restroom, bathing, sleeping, or changing clothes. This is a rule for children and grownups, so let's always keep our restroom and bedroom doors closed when we're in there so we can have privacy."

Some parents feel awkward about having conversations with infants or toddlers who are pre-verbal. They may believe that it's too much information to communicate. However, a child can articulate a parent's voice and tone even during pregnancy. Additionally, conversing with a child builds their vocal skills and their vocabulary, which ultimately aids in sounding out words and reading. Conversing with an infant or toddler about CSA is the same as conversing with the child when you want to teach him the rules of sharing, good manners, or how to say hello and goodbye. It is the same concept as reading to your child, even when he's not able to read and write himself. If the child is not too young to listen to a story, then they're not too young to begin CSA prevention training.

Talk to your toddler about proper and improper touch. Remind your child that sometimes they can't take care of their own body, so in those times it is proper for a parent, caregiver, or sibling to help with diaper-changing, applying diaper rash lotion, bathing, or wiping after toilet use, and that these touches are good and proper. Teach your child that it's also "good touch" to give and receive hugs or things like being lifted while playing or to sit together with trusted friends and family. But they should know that it's never okay for them to be forced to hug or be touched by anyone (even family) if it makes him uncomfortable. Teach your child about respect for peers and adults by asking for permission to give them a hug or kiss or to hold their hand, because not everyone feels comfortable with touch—even good touch. This teaches your child about consent and non-consent and creates a culture of love and respect within your family and circle of friends. It reassures your child that he is encouraged to talk to you about proper and improper touch and that he will be supported when he comes to you with any concern. It gives your child the autonomy to choose proper versus improper touch.

Remind your child that sometimes people look nice, but that doesn't mean they are nice, and that anyone can make bad choices with improper touch. Let your child know that you trust his instincts and that he has a right to be respected when he does not want body contact. Say to your child that improper bad touch is when people try to see and touch privates or show their privates, even if they are playing a game or tickling. Say to your child, "Always tell me or a trusted adult if someone tries to touch, grab, or tickle you and it makes you feel uncomfortable."

Explain to your child that if someone rubs or tickles or touches their body and it makes them feel uncomfortable or hurts, that they should tell immediately and tell them to stop. That they should say "No!" if anyone tries to play with or touch their privates, even if they say it's just a game. That if they don't feel comfortable with any touch, they should say that it's a family rule that we don't do that when someone says no. That we do not take photos of or do anything with each other's privates. Your child will learn that his saying no to uncomfortable body contact will be respected because it's a family rule. This is an especially good stage to train your child to say no because children love to say no at this age, and the directive will stay with him.

Toddler to Five Years – WILL, PURPOSE

Your child is continuing to develop spiritually, emotionally, and physically, all thanks to God and you! Your child is growing in social skills. Your child is still building autonomy and developing his self-esteem as he learns right from wrong, as well as *initiative* versus *guilt*. Using initiative means the child is allowed to interact and assert himself vocally, make decisions, and lead and/or engage in activities. If the child is not encouraged to be assertive and instead is ridiculed, criticized, or discouraged from speaking up or taking initiative, then the child develops guilt for asserting himself and being "difficult." Taking initiative in making decisions means learning right from wrong, which requires the child to work with his self-will/free will. The child can either choose his own will or to follow the rules (God's, parent's, or society's will).

This is a significant age group because children are exploring the world around them, observing, and making decisions about what it means to be an adult. You'll find them questioning adults and sometimes being conflicted with the parental and adult role, constantly asking, "Why?" When a parent is a responsible parent, there isn't much to explain or justify regarding the rules or why things are done. The parent may want to clarify that the rules fulfill a purpose. They may want to give an example of how the child using his mind to learn the rules keeps him and the family safe. If a child is well-learned, nourished, and nurtured during this stage, he will have established confidence instead of shame. He will feel that he has a purpose in this life, providing that you have taught body part names, including his genitals, without frightening him, and have gently explained that it's wrong for anyone to touch his private parts.

As a refresher, ask your child the names of all his body parts and ensure he understands. Calmly remind your child that the genitals are private and are not for displaying to others, taking photos of, or touching (other than to clean). Remind your child to say no if anyone asks him to touch their private parts. Children are vulnerable to sex offenders at these ages because they're vacillating between feeling proud of themselves with good self-esteem for their initiatives and achievements and low self-esteem or feelings of guilt and shame for their inability to grasp all skills without repeat tries.

Periodically have a light discussion on body safety, especially before your child will be out of your realm of supervision (birthday party sleepover, play date), just to keep a healthy communication going between the two of you. This may appear as an excessive focus on CSA but in the grand scheme of a child's and family's life this light hearted reminder is but a mild infusion into their overflowing schedules. If time passes and it's never talked about again, the child may no longer feel comfortable talking to you about it.

Say to your child that someone would probably never try to touch his private parts and that he doesn't need to spend time worrying about it, but you want to make sure he knows exactly what to do in case it ever happens. Teach your child by giving him several examples of the difference between inappropriate and appropriate touch.

Tell him that in the same way that he knows what to do if the toilet starts overflowing (tell a grownup), he needs to know what to do if anyone tries to inappropriately touch him. Ask your child to always tell right away if anyone ever tries to touch him or asks him to touch them inappropriately. You are giving your child the right to use initiative and to practice not feeling guilty if he has to tell on someone. You are giving the child the authority to not do anything against his will, to respectfully speak up, just like adults get to do.

Your child is adapting his social position within your family system and that role is one of having the right to assert himself and command respect of his body. Teach your child the difference between keeping a good and a bad secret. Tell him that if he keeps a bad secret, no one can help him. Ask your child never to promise anyone that he will keep a bad secret. Ask him what he will do if anyone asks him to keep a bad secret, like spending alone time with a "bad touch person." When he says that he would tell, praise him for his answer. Ask him what he would do if anyone tried to touch his private parts. Ask him what he would do if anyone asked him to touch someone else's private parts. Praise him when he says that he would tell.

Teach your child that only people who want to do bad touch ask for children to promise to keep their friendship a secret. Tell your child that he must say that his family has a no-secret rule, that his parent or caregiver must be told when someone asks him to promise to keep anything a secret. Tell him that a bad secret is like keeping a lie, and it makes everyone sad when the secret is found out. Give the child examples of when your family has kept a surprise a secret, but explain that that is a good and fun secret that will make everyone happy and is meant to be revealed in time. Train your child that his mouth is for eating, drinking, brushing his teeth, and flossing. Grownups can help with eating and cleaning, but no one is to touch or play with his mouth. Let your child know that this is a family rule as well, except when he goes to the dentist, and that you or the dental assistant will be standing by while the dentist examines his mouth.

Train your child that he is not allowed to accept any money, gifts, or special privileges without that person speaking to you or his caregiver first. Ask your child to say, "No, thank you. We have a family rule; no gifts without permission." Teach your child what the word bribe means and how some people use gifts to persuade children to do things they don't want to do. Tell your child that when a person does not say no, the other person thinks it's okay to offer gifts or do anything they want. Saying no or no thank you and having to have permission to do something teaches a child that the rule applies both at home and outside of the home and empowers him to be ready if he ever has to say no to someone.

Your child will learn that it's okay to say no to anyone, even an adult, without feeling bad about it. It also trains the child to trust his instincts if he feels uncomfortable about someone giving him gifts or privileges, wanting him to keep secrets, or trying to convince him to break family rules. This training opens the door to him telling you if he ever has to say no. Maintaining that open communication bond with your child is the first line of defense in preventing CSA.

Look for resources that can enhance your child's learning about body safety to supplement your CSA training, but remember that no matter how many lessons you verbalize in those teaching moments, the most important action you can take toward your child's body safety is your non-verbal role modeling, which demonstrates your love and respect for your child.

It's crucial to stay neutral and in a composed mood if your child voices his having been approached by an offender or if you begin to see signs of CSA, even if you are unsure if it may be a symptom of a non-CSA-related stressor. Allow your child to express his thoughts and feelings without your nervous or angry energy. This will allow for assessing the incident without making irrational or unfounded allegations/conclusions.

It is normal for a parent to feel both horrified and mortified when a child starts behaving in overly sexual ways, especially if they suspect that the child may have been abused. However, do not allow your negativity to show on your face in front of the child. Instead, look at him with compassion. Stay on neutral ground until the child has completely shared his thoughts and experiences. Then, tell the child how sorry you are that CSA happened to him, but that you will find a counselor to help. Then contact your local Child Advocacy Center hotline and ask for their assistance in determining the next steps, which can include calling the civil authorities.

Age Six to Twelve — COMPETENCE

The school-age child is mostly preoccupied with *industry* versus *inferiority*. At this stage, the child is capable of building a body of knowledge from academics to various areas of creativity and becomes skilled in whatever sources of interest he has, developing an *industrious* sense of self. Through his sense of industry, he can increase in confidence and competence. However, if the child experiences rejection or feelings of not being valued or validated, he will lose confidence and feel inadequate and *inferior*. Now the child is being critiqued by his social relationships (outside of parental relationship) at school, in the community, his church, etc.; his view of himself is influenced by their feedback and authority over him.

If the inferiority complex remains unresolved, confidence and competence are affected. The child may experience some mental health concerns. Through this social stage of development, the child becomes increasingly aware of the difference in boy and girl personalities and body parts. He might be inquisitive and ask questions about boy/girl or boyfriend/girlfriend relationships as well as mommy and daddy's relationship. He may even ask how babies are made. Some children ask this question at an earlier age due to curiosity or being prompted by seeing a pregnant woman or the good news that a sibling is on the way.

Always answer the child's questions in a relaxed way and in simple, short terms—the same manner the child *asks* questions. Do not refrain from answering human body development or basic human reproduction or sexuality questions, as you want your child to receive healthy, accurate answers from you without being exploited with excessive or inaccurate information by peers or the internet. No need to get flustered; it's actually a healthy opportunity to share what a wonderful gift the human body is and how (in basic terms) reproduction works.

Most children love to talk about animals. Children are fascinated that human females are mammals and have parts similar to many of the mammals they're learning about in science class. They are fascinated to know that females have tiny eggs and that sometimes one of those little eggs develops into a baby in the mommy's tummy and that that's why pregnant women and animals grow bigger bellies—because there's a baby inside!

If the child learns that the body is a beautiful creation from God, he will respect, be grateful for, and be happy about his body. If a child has already been taught to be comfortable talking about the human body, he will always feel at ease when he wants to talk about a concern with his own body.

This age group requires parents to have their CSA safety plan in gear more than before, because the child is now bombarded daily with the world's sexualized messages. The child has developed a higher level of attention span. Parents should monitor all media from television, to games, music, e-books, computers, phones, billboard roadways signs, magazines, books, and adult or peer attire and behaviors. It is your role to be the first to teach your child the values and principles God ordained for sex and relationships.

If you have offered open communication with your child about any subject matter and about life in general, be prepared for him to ask questions about sexual words, concepts, and relationships. The child may be perplexed or confused by the sexual behaviors in commercials, in electronic games, or in children's movies, which can introduce provocative dressing, dancing, or other inappropriate behaviors. The child's exposure to sources of inappropriate sexual behaviors can lead him to believe this is normal behavior, and he may mimic what he's seen or attempt to imitate these behaviors to relate to his peers.

Access to pornography becomes easier for a child at this stage. Parents must take action to protect all sources of media in the household and teach the child to stay away from others who attempt to show them any form of pornography. Teach the child the difference between a healthy, beautiful sexual relationship between husband and wife and how disturbing and traumatizing it is for people to use the human body and human sexuality—which God created—in a destructive, damaging way. Tell the child about the damage that pornography can cause children and adults, due in part to the spiritual, emotional, and physical abuse that takes place with pornography.

If your child has begun to speak on human development and sexuality in adult terms, it is very important to ask him where he's gotten this information. Explain in a non-exploitive way what pornography is, then ask the child about the possibility of him having been exposed to pornography. Some children are petrified to tell a parent about their experience with pornography and may refrain from telling them because they feel ashamed or think they will get in trouble because the pornography has stimulated them, and they feel guilty and at fault. Explain to your child that he will not get in trouble for sharing if he has been exposed to pornography.

Also provide a brief explanation that predators place the pornography in front of people's eyes because they know that the body is physically stimulated by sexual visual images, but he will not be punished for his body having a normal biological response. If the child refuses to disclose information or his source(s), it is helpful to involve a CSA-trained counselor to do a professional evaluation and to obtain a diagnosis with recommendations. Determine whether a local Child Advocacy Center needs to be notified regarding the child's suspected exposure to sexual behaviors.

If, after you have covered the media rules for your family, you notice your child acting out sexually without apparent provocation and he does not disclose exposure to pornography or another source, you must not let him continue to exhibit such behavior. Connect your child with a CSA therapist who can identify the source of his behavior and redirect him back to his pre-exposure healthy functioning. Not resolving this behavior will increase its occurrence. It could escalate to pornography or other sexual disorders and will not just affect him and your family, but could also affect all others who are in his circle.

Generally, when a child experiences CSA, he has not had the support from trusted adults with consistent education on body safety. A child who receives CSA safety training feels loved and cared for. If someone attempts to exploit a child who has not had CSA body safety training, he feels exploited, ashamed, and confused. He doesn't know how to speak about or how to comprehend what is happening to him. Just as children learn that rules exist everywhere, they also have to be taught rules about their bodies and the rights they have regarding how they are treated.

The message sent to the CSA-trained child is that CSA safety has to be taught and learned. When a child is not told about the dangers of CSA and he discovers them on his own, he thinks the parents or caregivers just don't talk about those things or that they forgot to tell him. In these cases, he's more likely to not tell the secret.

If you've missed the mark on training your child and protecting him from CSA, it's never too late to reclaim your role and recommit to your responsibility. Do not condemn yourself, as there is no condemnation in Christ (Romans 8:1). Ask God for His forgiveness on neglecting your parental duties and just say out loud to yourself that from this moment on, you will meet this responsibility. God's relentless, forgiving Spirit and compassion, which is renewed every morning, always allows us to start afresh!

> *Through the Lord's mercies we are not consumed, because His compassions fail not. They are new every morning; great is Your faithfulness. "The Lord is my portion," says my soul, "Therefore I hope in Him!"* (Lamentations 3:22-24).

In God's divine agenda, a thousand years is the same as a day. That means He can make up for lost time, because a day is a thousand years to Him. Think about how much you can accomplish in training up your child if you start today. Today, according to God's laws of time, you can accomplish a thousand years of quality teaching time with your child! Pray along with Moses, as he prayed to God for His people: *So teach us to number our days, that we may gain a heart of wisdom* (Psalm 90:12).

Always be mindful that when God and His agenda are involved, a little purposeful time spent with Him or your child is a lot of time in His eyes and on His timeline. However, our busiest, most stressful workdays are not worth a minute of our godless days. When we are not doing what we are called to do with God's time, we operate under godless days, and we waste a lot of precious time: *For a thousand years in Your sight are like yesterday when it is past, and like a watch in the night* (Psalm 90:4).

If your child questions or mentions discomfort with your sudden attention, it's a very healthy approach to admit that you've made a mistake by neglecting this responsibility. It is as simple as saying, "I am sorry I was not available as a parent in teaching you and helping you out with questions you may have had or things you may have been going through. I was wrong. From now on, I want to be and will be available to answer any questions and to guide you. I want to always be there for you when you need me. Will you forgive me?"

Sometimes your child won't readily forgive because of a begrudging heart or fears that you can't be trusted to follow through with your promise. No worries; just pray for him to come around to believing and trusting you. In time, through your *consistent* and responsible parenting, he will see and feel your renewed commitment and sense your love for him. Love is an action word that, especially with broken spirits, must be actively demonstrated.

> *Love suffers long and is kind; love does not envy; love does not parade itself, is not puffed up; does not behave rudely, does not seek its own, is not provoked, thinks no evil; does not rejoice in iniquity, but rejoices in the truth; bears all things, believes all things, hopes all things, endures all things. Love never fails. And now abide faith, hope, love, these three; but the greatest of these is love* (1 Corinthians 13:4-8,13).

Right before you each week is an opportunity for your child to receive support and to supplement the godly principles you're teaching him. It's church! Your child can become equipped to deal with daily challenges by attending church and learning through God's Word. Most churches have children's ministries by age groups, vacation bible schools, camps, and other programs. As a part of your child safety screening approach, make sure it's a Bible-teaching church and not a cult, such as those that use books besides the Bible to minister. There is no book needed other than the Bible to learn God's principles. Obviously, it's fine if it's an educational or inspirational book that uses biblical scripture to teach God's Word and encourage, but it is not to be used as an equal to or substitute for the Bible.

The reason it's not necessary to read any other book for God's guidance is because the Bible was sent from God directly through the power of the Holy Spirit (who dwelt in the holy hearts of all of those God called to write the manuscripts). God's Spirit moved holy men of God to write His Word. The entire Bible is infallible and inerrant because it came directly from God's inspiration through the Holy Spirit, and since God the Father and the Holy Spirit are a perfect, sinless deity, there can be no error in God's Word. The Bible is God's direct voice speaking to us through the power of the Holy Spirit. As we read it, we become equipped with His instructions and guidance.

> *All Scripture is given by inspiration of God, and is profitable for doctrine, for reproof, for correction, for instruction in righteousness, that the man of God may be complete, thoroughly equipped for every good work* (2 Timothy 3:16-17).

> *Knowing this first, that no prophecy of Scripture is of any private interpretation, for prophecy never came by the will of man, but holy men of God spoke as they were moved by the Holy Spirit* (2 Peter 1:20-21).

If you take a child to a non-Bible-teaching church, you are essentially teaching him to worship another God, because all other books written and followed by a church are manmade thoughts and *not* inspired by the Holy Spirit. If it's not written in the Bible, do not believe it. Do not lead your child astray by believing content man has added through other books that a church uses on equal par with or as a substitute for the Bible.

God's Word is very direct about the consequence for anyone who attempts to add, revise, or remove contents from His Word. In Revelation 22:18-19, He says: *For I testify to everyone who hears the words of the prophecy of this book: If anyone adds to these things, God will add to him the plagues that are written in this book; and if anyone takes away from the words of the book of this prophecy, God shall take away his part from the Book of Life, from the holy city, and from the things which are written in this book."*

It is important to attend church, because while you can grow spiritually by reading God's Word on your own, God also calls us to assemble together to worship Him in fellowship with one another (Ephesians 4:11-13, Romans 10:17, Colossians 3:16, Hebrews 10:24-25, Acts 9:31, Matthew 16:18 and 18:20, James 1:22). Attending church supplements, encourages, and strengthens your spiritual growth and helps you maintain a consistent relationship with God and other fellow Christians. That's why your church is called a church home, and the brothers and sisters who attend with you are called your church family. Accepting salvation is the first step to a relationship with Christ. Growing in Christ is the next!

After you have done your research on a Bible-teaching church, it goes without saying that a church is not exempt from your screening it for functional staff to lead the programs with body safety policies in place.

Age Twelve to Eighteen — FIDELITY

This psychosocial stage is *Identity* versus *Role Confusion*. The previous psychosocial stages of development are dependent on what is done for and to the child. This adolescent stage is dependent on what the child does.

The child is now a teenager challenged by the search for his own *identity*. This age group struggles with balancing their social interactions, sometimes negotiating and compromising in order to fit in while in the meantime differentiating between right and wrong and developing morality. Some adolescents become overwhelmed by this stage and take a moratorium from responsibilities, withdrawing or acting out and attempting to delay becoming an adult. This in turn creates turmoil and *role confusion*.

If the adolescent is successful in returning to his responsible, well-grounded role with a sense of identity and purpose, he will reconnect with his foundation of relationships, ideals, and causes, and become devoted to that foundation with fidelity. This makes the adolescent's entrance into adulthood productive and purposeful. If the adolescent leaves this stage unresolved, the results are serious mental health consequences leading into adulthood.

The spiritual, emotional, and physical growth of this age range is moving more rapidly than ever with the individual values and principles taught, becoming the foundation of his being. The adolescent's mind, more so than in previous ages, is discerning what constitutes right from wrong or amoral decisions. This is a prime time for parents to teach their child accountability and good decision making, both when they are in the presence of others and when they're alone. Teach them that their decisions should be well thought out and solid. A solid decision is one in which they have considered the consequences and understand that the choices made not only affect themselves and their own lives but also their loved ones' and others' around them. They should understand that these decisions could impact them and others for a lifetime.

There is a very vulnerable phase during which the adolescent is learning about romance and making decisions about relationships with peers, adults, school grades, and goals. This phase challenges his self-esteem and how he views himself in his standing with others. The same risks for exploitation of sexuality exist within this group as with the pre-adolescent ages of nine to twelve, but at a more intense and faster pace (e.g., the opportunities for premarital sex, more activities promoting access to sexual predators, sexting, online chatting with potential sex offenders, date rape, and voyeurism). This age group strives to be independent of the parent in every area of their life, including human sexuality. However, unless the parent allows the adolescent to take over the parental role in the family, the instruction about everything in life, including CSA, continues, and the adolescent highly benefits from the parent's healthy empathic teachings, protection, and modeled influence.

Peer pressure is reduced when a child grows up in a church environment with peers that have learned about God's love being equally the same for everyone and that no one is better than another. Bullying is reduced as well, because the church teaches God's principles to love one another. Your child can find godly peers for encouragement during the tough middle and high school years through youth ministry groups, church camps, and special boys or girls ministry events that discourage drug and alcohol use and encourage purity of the body.

There are special purity events held around the country that present human sexuality to tweens and teens through God's principles. They're open to parents and, during these events, many of the pre-adolescents/adolescents in attendance offer to make a commitment to body purity. They then wear a ring as a reminder of their commitment to purity until marriage. This event teaches and supports what the parent is teaching: that Christ will be honored through their body when they keep it pure and away from the temptation of sin.

The research shows that most adolescents are actually relieved by the messages taught in youth group ministries and purity events. They're relieved that they don't have to make the decision about sexual relations now and can wait until that special godly person comes into their life and they get married. Check with your church or the internet for the location of the nearest upcoming teen purity event.

During this time, as in others, it's important that you don't have a double standard and that you walk your talk. Don't expect your tween or teen to attend church if you're sleeping in on Sundays, going to church but never reading God's Word, or only going once per week but not continuing to spiritually feed yourself as you expect your child to do. There are small church groups, Bible studies, and men's/women's ministry events you can attend, not just to role model but also to grow spiritually yourself. There are some fun Bible teaching events you can find information for on the internet which are designed for parents to attend with their children. Some are even specifically designed for fathers to attend with their sons and mothers to attend with their daughters. These events will help you both grow in Christ. If you don't want to surf the internet for parent-child church events, call your local Christian radio station. They usually have a calendar of upcoming concerts and family and parent-child events.

The research shows that one of the reasons this age group gets into trouble is that before they take on their first job and sometimes even after, they have too much time on their hands. That time is usually spent either learning the values of their social media connections or getting involved in destructive activities. Most churches introduce the idea of serving the community and others outside of the community doing missions work. This gives tweens and teens an opportunity to think outside of their own selves (most humans are born selfish, and that selfishness increases during adolescence).

Missions outings with the church provide the virtue of empathy for others who are not as blessed. Missions also teach the act of being grateful for blessings. And when adolescents focus on others instead of themselves, they don't have time to get involved with vices and the negative aspects of a digital world that wants to lure them into an "it's all about me" culture. There's already sufficient peer pressure at school and in the media. You and the church can teach your child that he doesn't have to feel pressured to submit to material things, inappropriate fashion, or a sexualized culture in order to feel confident and good about himself.

Explain to your adolescent that wanting to be someone besides themselves for the sake of fitting in or feeling more confident is not in God's plan for their Spirit, Mind, or Body. Teach him the definition of manipulation and how peers and adults can manipulate to get others to do what they want. Remind your child that he is one of God's unique creations and that there's no one on earth who's exactly like him. He is designed by God's Hand and in God's Image, produced and perfected to grow up to become like just like Him. Knowing this ought to make him feel good about being himself. This knowledge should raise his self-esteem and improve His confidence in being proud of who and what he is—uniquely created by His Highness, the King of Kings, His personal Designer!

No one ever has peace about or feels happy about being someone they're not, especially when they've changed to please others. Teach your child that because he is not separate from God in His Image, he must welcome and allow God into every part of His life. By doing so, he will learn to reflect God's Image and character. Remind him that if he chooses to keep God out of his life, God is still present, because no one can hide from God:

> And there is no creature hidden from His sight, but all things are naked and open to the eyes of Him to whom we must give account (Hebrews 4:13).

Share with your child that he will only find peace and happiness when he fulfills God's expectation for him to be his own unique self—the one he was created to be—and when he takes good care of that self. He must take care of himself because the Spirit, Mind, and Body God gave uniquely to him does not belong to anyone else to make his choices—it belongs to God and him alone. Explain to your child that it is a sin to reject or harm the body God created and that our body is His gift to us:

> *Or do you not know that your body is the temple of the Holy Spirit who is in you, whom you have from God, and you are not your own?...therefore glorify God in your body and in your spirit, which are God's* (1 Corinthians 6:19-20).

Remind your child that when he introduces sin into his body, it not only brings grief to himself (instead of peace), but it also grieves God's Spirit, because He created and designed our bodies for good purposes. Share this verse with him: *And do not grieve the Holy Spirit of God* (Ephesians 4:30).

An adolescent is a child who is still developing spiritually, neurologically, emotionally, and physically. When an adult CSA predator manipulates an adolescent and disguises himself as being interested in the child romantically (to cover up his real intent for a sexual relationship), it is against the law, and charges of statutory rape can be filed. Some predators end up manipulating their victim into marriage, and victims have been known to leave their families for the predator. Some of these victims become educated on CSA as adults and realize then that they were lured into CSA.

It doesn't make it easier for an adolescent to discover that they are being sexually abused simply because they are older, nor does their chronological age indicate that they will be more likely to disclose the secret. Most of the time, the emotional impairment and consequences of the abuse prevent this age group from telling. This age group is, in fact, more at risk for engaging in self-defeating behaviors and needs extra help to stay safe from their own self-destructive ways. This is why the strong line of communication is priceless with children, because that connection can remain strong well into adolescence and can be very useful during a CSA crisis. Adolescents still need a parent or caregiver to make the report—chances are very slim that they will make a self-report, even if they have a cell phone.

Unfortunately, a cell phone, which is meant to be helpful, can work against children. And even when a parent works hard to supervise a phone, they're getting increasingly difficult to monitor because technology keeps improving the ways that the cellphone owner can block others from tracking the phone's location or the ability for apps to hide certain content. The best effort a parent can make is to pay for a basic cell phone service that only allows phone calling and no internet service. However, there still remains the serious problem of sexting between peers and, at times, the exploitation of CSA via texting apps. Regardless of whether the parent or the adolescent is paying for the cell phone service, it is still the responsibility of the parent or caregiver to protect their child from CSA. The best resolve is to make cell phone and electronic devices a part of the Body Safety Family Plan and to incorporate rules into the plan for responsible phone and social device use.

Adolescence marks a rite of passage into the work world. As a teenager, your child may become employed, and you can't assume that because having a job is a responsible step that everyone else around them will act responsibly. No matter the job they take, your job as a parent is not over. Your responsibility has now increased—you must make sure your child has done his homework, checking out his employer's policies on sexual harassment and CSA protection of employees.

Some parents think that adolescents are not at risk for sexual harassment, but consider the following: if adult of various ages have experienced sexual harassment through uninvited hugs and bodily pats from coworkers and employers, why would your adolescent be excluded from those workplace risks? It doesn't matter if the employer is a family member or close friend of the family, the place of employment must still be a place where the child feels safe, and any discomfort must be immediately addressed with the employer or coworker and reported to the parent.

It is not out of place for a parent to screen the new employer's or the organization's background before the child agrees to work there. This becomes yet another teaching moment for the parent to bring awareness to their teen about the existence of sexual harassment and CSA in the workplace. It is a great time to review body safety precautions. Most likely, the new job has a reputable employer with safety policies in place. And, more than likely, they are prudent about the staff they hire. But it doesn't hurt to do background checks and screenings when it comes to protecting your child from CSA.

No matter how disrespectful and challenging an adolescent becomes in reaction to their parents instructions and decisions, it does not release the parent from the responsibility of staying ever so consistent in the prevention and protection education and the requirement that they honor household rules, values, and principles. Research has documented evidence that, neurologically, even if it appears that a teen is not caring or listening to their parent, the brain memory bank proves otherwise (God's role, values, principles, parental concern, and advice is in storage). So keep that open-door policy, because your children—at all age levels—are listening. Even if they don't appear to be registering any of the information, they are.

Children need to be heard as well. Do you want to know what your child is thinking? Listen to them speak about the world they live in. *Their* world. In addition to them listening to your instruction, listen to them as well. Each stage of psychosocial development presents a different set of joyful and difficult times for them to experience and work through, both in the home and outside it. Be there for them every step of the way.

Your opportunity to teach and train up your child is brief and momentary. There are many timeless things in this world we can always come back to, but this is not one of them. When it comes to raising children, time is not timeless. It goes by quickly. When the Bible describes life as a vapor, it's not just talking about how it passes us by quickly. It is reminding us that there are opportunities in our lives which God provides that we must realize we cannot return to.

Each of your child's psychosocial developmental stages will phase in, phase down, and phase out, without them giving you notice. Without them batting an eyelash, they will move forward, whether you've trained them well or not, into the next developmental stage. Quality time with children has been touted as an ideal in raising upright children (especially when both parents work outside of the home). However, that is not the case with CSA training. CSA training requires both quantity and quality time from the parent. Be patient and always mindful to teach children at their own pace. Sometimes you may give the quantity of time, but your child is tired or inattentive and distracted by other items on their agenda. When this happens, and when the subject is important, you may have to wait for the most opportune time to speak with them.

Never feel guilty when you have missed an opportunity to speak to your child because your schedule unexpectedly changed for an equally urgent matter. God is a God of perfect timing, and if you're committed to spending time with your child, God will urge another opportunity for you to make up that lost time. He is the author of time and the God of perfect timing!

What you *do* or *do not do* during your child's psychosocial developmental stages strongly affects whether they master the concepts of that stage, as well as those virtues you have taught them. Sure, they may choose to use their free will and to not internalize your CSA training, but at the very least you can rest your head at night knowing you have been a responsible parent and that you have accepted the opportunity and privilege given to you to teach your child God's principles and healthy body behavior.

Your child will be living at home during five out of eight of the psychosocial developmental stages. Once they phase out of stage five, they're no longer a minor. And even if they're still living at home past stage five, your window of opportunity to teach them will have slipped away, because during and after stage five it is more about what *they* do that influences their life and less about what *you* do to train them. Past stage five, it is all about what you have already done and what they choose to do with it.

Parenting responsibly through the psychosocial stages and adding CSA training on top of that may seem like an overwhelming calling. But if you take a moment *right now* to receive it as an opportunity to overcome any world or family dysfunction which your child may be or may have been exposed to, then you, your child, your family, and others will reap the benefits, even into future generations. Commit right now to responsible parenting throughout all of the psychosocial stages and include CSA training in that package deal!

Whereas you do not know what will happen tomorrow. For what is your life? It is even a vapor that appears for a little time and then vanishes away (James 4:14).

PART II
BECOMING AWARE OF CSA AND IMPLEMENTING SAFETY

All your children shall be taught by the Lord, and great shall be the peace of your children. In righteousness you shall be established; you shall be far from oppression, for you shall not fear; and from terror, for it shall not come near you.

Isaiah 54:13-14

Focus on Safety: What to DO

There is a huge difference between *saying* that child safety is a primary concern and actually taking the steps make it so. Watching your children requires your undivided attention when it comes to CSA, but it also takes knowing what to look for.

Sex offenders have been known to improperly touch children right before the parent's eyes. If, for example, your eyes are on your electronic device, you may not notice that a medical professional is improperly touching your child right in front of you. Yes, sexual predators are that unbounded and self-entitled in helping themselves to children. Focusing on safety requires the truth be known, faced, and accepted—that *all* adults, youth, and peers around the child who are believed to be good people are capable of sexually abusing the child. This truth is based on the evidence that in most cases children have been abused by respected adults or family or peers who are never suspected. The fact that adults are often well-respected and carry authority and power only increases the likelihood that more child victims will be impacted and will report CSA cases less often. Even more, parents and other adults often feel intimidated, threatened, or powerless over CSA and the adult predator. But it is the parent's duty to investigate those who will be around the child so that the child is not compromised. It is their responsibility to deter those prospective predators that can be by simply addressing the safety concern.

CSA prevention is most effective when it is addressed first within the family system. Child sexual abuse lives in family systems from one generation to another when the family lacks the fortitude to become aware and address it. The following are some child sexual abuse awareness tips:

Child Sexual Abuse Awareness Tips:

✓ Do not deny that the greatest risk for CSA comes from those you and the child know.

✓ Teach your child his body parts and respect for his and others' bodies.

✓ Teach your child the difference between consensual and nonconsensual body touch.

✓ Educate yourself on the sex abuser profile and grooming characteristics.

✓ Be transparent about your expectations of others' behavior around your child.

✓ Reduce all opportunities and access to your child for CSA.

✓ Screen ALL the people that will be working with your child for his childcare or extracurricular activities.

✓ Learn about CSA and the protocol for CSA reporting and mental health/medical treatment.

✓ Have open discussions and scheduled family talks for everyone to be likeminded on the definition of inappropriate touch. Realize that there may be parents and caregivers who are offenders or are ignoring and enabling abuse. It's urgent that CSA info be disseminated to all adults in the child's life so that the child can have a support system of trusted adults.

✓ Always trust you and your child's instincts for discomfort around people or circumstances.

✓ Be vigilant if it appears that your child is being singled out (whether favored or oppressed), as it places your child at risk.

✓ If you are aware of an offender, do not enable the child to be abused by allowing the offender's presence at family or extracurricular activities. The offender's presence not only puts your child at risk, but can disempower him by making him feel unsafe.

Focus on Safety: What NOT to Do

✓ Do not forego discussing CSA with your child for fear of frightening him.

✓ Do not trust people totally based on their well-respected profiles in the community.

✓ Do not trust schools or organizations to teach the child body safety.

✓ Do not trust schools or organizations to have in place CSA educational programs for staff.

✓ Do not trust schools or organizations to have established CSA policies/programs for children.

✓ Do not assume that your child will be safe at a peer's or family member's sleepover if you haven't screened the environment, hosts, and attendees.

✓ Do not assume that because it's family or a good friend doing the childcare that they're above reproach.

✓ Do not declare that incest could never happen in your family. Denying and never discussing the reality that incest exists only produces ignorance in the child, places him at risk, and enables its occurrence. A child with a lack of awareness cannot prevent or protect himself.

Body Safety Guide

❖ Teach your child that his body belongs to God Who created it, and it is a gift to him. It is the child's private property. Tell your child that he has a right to say no if he's uncomfortable with anyone touching him.

❖ Teach your child the biological names for all his body parts, including his private parts.

❖ Instruct your child which parts of his body are private and that his private parts are to always be covered except when bathing or at a medical exam and in the presence of you or another parent or caretaker.

❖ Teach your child as early as toddlerhood that he's not to look at, touch, play with, or hurt anyone's private parts.

❖ Make sure your child is aware that there are people who are not to be trusted because they break the "no touch" body safety rule for private parts.

❖ Teach your child the body safety rule that he is never to keep any bad secrets from his parent or circle of trusted adults, including private parts secrets.

❖ Ask your child to always tell right away if someone attempts to break one of their body safety rules.

❖ Teach your child that it is never too late to tell if someone has broken one of their body safety rules.

❖ Instruct your child not to give up on telling a trusted adult until he is helped.

❖ Reassure your child that it is an adult's responsibility to keep him safe.

❖ Tell your child that somebody touching or forcing him to touch someone is not their fault.

❖ Create a body safety plan using the rules in this safety guide. Share your family's body safety plan with caregivers, family, friends, professionals, and whoever your child has contact with. These people become your child's *body safety circle*, and can oversee his safety when he's away from you. They are people the child says he would feel comfortable telling about a CSA concern.

❖ As part of a body safety plan, the child must develop, together with a parent or caregiver, a list of trusted adults whom he can call to ask questions or talk to when he has body safety concerns if for any reason you're not available.

What to DO to Reduce the Risks Created by Devices & Social Media

✓ Be savvy about setting up filters for explicit images/language content on computers, phones, etc.

✓ Check browsing history and inspect apps to be certain inappropriate contents are not being concealed.

✓ Keep all electronic devices in visible, common areas of the home.

✓ All electronic devices must be time-limited at age-appropriate levels.

✓ All electronic devices must be off limits and turned off overnight.

✓ If you allow your child social media, you're the best supervisor to follow his online safety. Be sure the privacy settings are set so that only those whom he chooses and whom you agree upon can interact with him. Always check that your child is not restricting what you see.

✓ Younger children benefit from not including their last name online and minimizing personal identification information on social media accounts.

✓ Warn your child that complete anonymity on the internet is a myth and impossible.

✓ Talk to your child about the dangers of online chatting with strangers or accepting unknown friend requests on social media, and give examples.

✓ Explain to your child that there are adult CSA predators on the internet pretending to be peers.

✓ Tell your child the CSA rule of never sending inappropriate images online (give examples of such both with clothes on and without), even to friends. Teach your child that creating digital or hard copy nude images (selfies or of other minors) in suggestive sexual poses, whether as a joke or not, is a crime.

✓ Tell your child about the legal consequences for sending or receiving nude images of underage minors on the internet.

✓ Tell your child to use internet safety rules because one out of five children report CSA solicitation online.

✓ Explain to your child that sending anything inappropriate through the internet becomes a part of his record and can be seen whenever anyone looks up his name (including future employers).

✓ Discuss with your child the importance of never giving out or sending personal identifying information (phone number, email, home address, etc.) on social media, even to friends.

What to DO to Reduce the Risk of Pornography Use

In 2013, the University of New Hampshire conducted a study through the Crimes Against Children Research Center and posted an article entitled, "The Complex Experience of Child Pornography Survivors." The study was done by Ateret Gewirtz-Meydan, Wendy Walsh, Janis Wolak, and David Finkelhor. In that study, the United States federal and state statutes for child pornography (CP) were posted with their full definition, laws, and other substantial CP studies. The following is an excerpt from the study, which defines child pornography according to U.S. laws:

Pornography has become a serious problem in the United States and worldwide, fostered by the development of online and digital technologies (Wolak, Finkelhor, & Mitchell, 2011; Wolak, Liberatore, &Levine, 2014). According to the Federal statutes, CP is the visual depiction . . . of sexually explicit conduct (18 USCS 2256) involving persons under age eighteen. Sexually explicit conduct includes acts such as intercourse, lascivious exhibition of the genitals or pubic area. Because the federal statute defines child to include sixteen and seventeen-year-old teenagers, youth under eighteen who can legally consent to sexual intercourse (age sixteen and older in most states) cannot consent to being photographed in sexually explicit poses. Further, adults who persuade or induce minors to create sexually explicit images are generally considered CP producers. Many states mirror federal law, although there is some variation in the definition of child and the content that is proscribed. Arrests for crimes involving CP production have more than quadrupled between 2000 and 2009. The growth is largely attributable to cases of "youth produced sexual images" solicited from minors by adult offenders and, despite the increase in youth produced sexual images, most CP producers arrested in 2009 were adults (Wolak, Finkelhor, & Mitchell, 2012). Youth-produced sexual images (often called sexting) add to the challenges of legislative systems which deal with child pornography prosecutions and arrests. Leukfeldt, Jansen, and Stol (2014) analyzed 159 Dutch police files related to images of abuse and exploitation child pornography and found that almost a quarter of the suspects were under twenty-four years of age. Of that group, 35% were younger than eighteen years.

Notice that the studies include overseas statistics. Pornography does not have to originate via the U.S. It is both an American *and* a worldwide problem, and can be transmitted internationally to a child in the U.S. in seconds. For added clarification, the U.S. code's definition of child pornography as it relates to digital technology is as follows:

Any visual image depiction of sexually explicit conduct involving a minor (child eighteen years of age or younger): Visual image depictions include digital or computer-generated images indistinguishable from an actual minor; images created, adapted, or modified, but appear to depict an identifiable, actual minor. Photographs: digital or hard copy, and videos. Federal law prohibits and considers under the law any undeveloped film/videotape, to be stored electronically to convert into a visual image the same as a visual depiction. It is important to note that the Federal law's definition of sexually explicit conduct does not require that a CP image show a child engaging in sexual activity. An image of a nude child can be defined as the crime of CP if it depicts a child in a sexually compromised suggestive pose. Also worthy of noting is that the child's age of consent is insignificant according to state law: the visual depiction of any child under the age of eighteen engaging in sexually explicit conduct is a crime.

Child pornography (CP), also called child sexual abuse images by professionals and researchers, has been found to have trauma implications beyond a child's sexual development. CP involves online (through the internet) or offline materials (like magazines, books, or movies). A research study conducted by the University of New Hampshire at the Crimes Against Children Research Center collected data the fall of 1999 and spring of 2000. The following is a synopsis of the conclusions:

Results from the current study suggest that among young, regular Internet users, those who report intentionally seeking pornography may be facing multiple challenges, including delinquent behavior and substance use. Further, there is an increased trend for youth who report clinical features of depression to be more likely to report online seeking versus offline-only seeking behavior. Thus, intentional exposure to pornography may be one behavior among many for young people struggling in their adolescence. Child and adolescent health professionals, and others interacting with youth should be sensitive to the possibility that at least for some young people, seeking out pornography either online or offline, has implications beyond their sexual development. Further, online seekers versus offline seekers are more likely to report clinical features associated with depression and lower levels of emotional bonding with their caregiver.

CP research has revealed that viewing pornography is an activity that not only results in traumatic and legal consequences, but both adults and children are at risk for becoming addicted. The findings stipulate that inviting, encouraging, exposing and/or allowing a child to view pornography promotes violence and sexual assault as a normal and aspired form of sexual behavior. Pornography viewers receive the message that the violent sexual behaviors exhibited are just a variety of sexual behaviors to explore and choose from. They desensitize the idea that sexual relations can include violent acts which are welcomed. Many offenders are taught from watching pornography that the painful response from their victims is the desired result, and they fulfill their violent fantasies with them.

Another study done at the Crimes Against Children Research Center by the University of New Hampshire concluded that almost all boys and two-thirds of girls over age thirteen have had exposure to online pornography. It was found that the solicitation or seeking of pornography takes place between the ages of fourteen and seventeen and that thousands of children under the age of thirteen are exposed *daily* to sexually explicit images. The findings identified boys as more likely to seek out pornography while girls were more likely to be involuntarily exposed to it.

In addition to the experience of trauma after regular exposure to pornographic images, pornography teaches children to take human sexuality out of context. Instead of the context of what God intended, a child is exposed to sexual relations from a pornographic perspective, which is contrary to His perspective. Sexual relations post-pornographic exposure are no longer seen through God's plan of intimacy between consenting adults within the context of a marital relationship. God's plan for sexual intimacy was purposely designed to protect and promote health and safety within the marital relationship. Pornography distorts and dissolves God's plan by introducing a child to an archive of corrupt memory files of human sexuality.

Pornography influences the child to view the adults and children participating in sexual behaviors as a normal process of human sexuality. The child believes the images he sees are valid representations of appropriate sexual behavior before he has any information files on healthy, God-ordained, intimate human sexuality. The child's first experience with human sexuality will affect his perception of human sexuality and future experiences. For instance, not all pornography involves sexual violence, but a lot of it does. The child will learn sexual behaviors and act on what he has viewed accordingly.

If he sees non-consenting adults having sexual relations, he will assume that consent is not necessary, even in his marriage. If he views pornography that shows unmarried people engaged in sexual relations openly and without respect, love, warmth, and affection, then he will not believe that privacy and those deep feelings are necessary for an intimate, godly marital relationship. Regardless of the type of pornography he views, his mind will be affected. In addition, his sexual behavior will be influenced while he's watching. It will affect his health and safety. Eventually it will impact others in his life.

So what is a parent to *do*? Protect, protect, protect! The internet is packed with state-of-the-art technological resources to filter and block anyone from access to pornography in the home, schools, and at places of employment. Use those resources! Just as a responsible parent's job is to prevent the sex offender from gaining access to the child, they are to do the same with all electronic devices—protect your child by not allowing them access to pornography.

Purchase filtering and blocking software for your home computers and devices. If using a library computer it's vital for the adult accompanying the child to first check with the library what their policy is on pornography filters. The federal government offers a subsidy to schools and libraries if they filter pornography. Not all libraries accept the subsidy some elect not to use filters. Schools use filters and blockers but that doesn't stop the pornography industry from using state of the art technology to infiltrate their porn agenda. Protecting your child's digital life may include purchasing software packages, setting up spam filters, and managing browsers and parental controls on all of your household's devices, but it's a worthwhile investment in your child and others.

If you're not technology-savvy, take a course to improve your skills. Some libraries have a technology department with staff that offer adult technology courses or who can assist you with specific questions about filtering and blocking software.

Will all this take time? Absolutely! And the faster you get on board, the faster you can get on track with protecting your child from the sexual images he'll be confronted with each day.

Will using filtering and blocking software guarantee cyberpornography safety for your child? Nope. Sad to say, but no software or app is foolproof because the providers of CP and adult pornography and *determined seekers* of pornography can sometimes work around filters and blockers. The most effective prevention and protection for your child from pornography is you. Yes, you. Software and apps are never to be used as babysitters or substitutes for an absent parent. It's back to consistent, traditional, and responsible parenting! Protecting your child from sexual images takes an active and a proactive parent.

The Body Safety Family Plan opens the door to normal discussion about God's plan for human sexuality and the dangers of offline and online pornography. If your child is uncomfortable discussing pornography as a part of the Body Safety Family Plan, reassure him that the body safety plan is just like an insurance policy; it is there for the sake of a protection plan. Explain to your child the truth about pornography, that it is filled with distorted, fictional depictions of sexual relations which have nothing to do with love and intimacy in a marital relationship.

Discuss the consequences of pornography with your child at an age-appropriate level. Share your family's values on pornography and human sexuality. This is just another safety hazard that can be added to the others that are articulated as body safety rules on the family plan. Explain to your child how, through the family policies on the body safety plan, he will reap lifetime benefits. Give examples of how a God-honoring child who understands God's plan for human sexuality reaps not just God's approval, but also a life of joy without the consequences of pornography in their present and future.

What to DO to Reduce the Risk of Child Sexual Abuse

- Parents can teach their infant and toddler children the proper names for their genitals (privates) while they teach the names of other body parts.

- Parents can teach their children that no one has a right to touch any part of their body if they don't want to be touched and that they can say "No!" to body touch that makes them uncomfortable.

- Children can be taught to respect and not to touch other people's bodies.

- Parents must be mindful and screen any adult who offers to do free childcare, to take the child on outings, or who brings special gifts for the child.

- Be careful who watches your children. Just because it's a sibling or relative doesn't make it the wisest or safest choice.

- Parents must research daycare or other childcare programs and feel welcome to attend activities and they must have an open-door policy in place for parents.

- Teach your children early that your home is a safe environment to talk about anything they're happy or upset about. Tell your children that it's okay to talk about sexual matters. Use every opportunity on the news as an example to begin discussing street smarts and body safety with them.

- Reiterate to your children that there is no subject they cannot discuss with you and to never keep bad secrets from their parents or caregivers. Tell your child that keeping a bad secret is breaking body safety rules.

- Remind your children that their entire body is private. They should always tell if anyone is violating their privacy by touching them in ways that make them uncomfortable.

- Parents can minimize their child's exposure to sexual abuse by being available to supervise him and by having a screened, trusted adult help monitor his relationships and whereabouts.

- Keeping your child at lower risk for sexual abuse includes limiting his accessibility—for instance, not publicizing his information on social media and not printing his name on outerwear or backpacks.

- Teach your child street smarts, like not walking alone to or from the bus stop and not talking to strangers unless he needs help. If he needs help, and only then, he should ask a woman with children to call the police.

- Have a Body Safety Family Plan in place.

- Make children a priority. A parent's, caregiver's, or community's silence gives sex offenders permission to violate vulnerable, impressionable children. All adults are capable of protecting children from sexual abuse by speaking up and learning the basic action steps to advocate against CSA.

All families are uniquely created by God. I hardly need say that a Body Safety Family Plan can differ strategically in some areas of concern and depending on the ages and personalities of each member involved. What remains the same is that the characteristics/tactics of the sexual predator don't change, and the goal to prevent CSA and protect the child from predators is the same for all families. Developing a Body Safety Family Plan can be an arduous task for some families, either because of their busyness or because they find the venture stressful or unpleasant. Consequently, some parents and caregivers procrastinate and never get around to creating the body safety plan. But if such is the case, consider the fact that Americans develop fire drill, tornado and hurricane, and mass shooting safety escape plans. So why not a body safety escape plan? A body safety plan is equally as important to teach children.

A parent or caregiver is charged by God with the honor and responsibility of authority and is held accountable for the care and safety of the child. They are at the helm of duty and are liable if they are not watching over the child. The purpose of a body safety plan is to resist and say no to child sexual abuse. To stamp out CSA! A Body Safety Family Plan means that the parent or caregiver has taken the time to educate themselves on what they need to know to keep the child safe and on how to help the community with the social problem of child sexual abuse.

The Body Safety Family Plan that follows is a basic example consisting of strategies, which can be eliminated if already completed or do not apply. It is open-ended for families to add to it their own safety goals:

Body Safety Family Plan

➢ A parent/caregiver must be alert, oversee, and supervise both the appropriate and inappropriate behaviors observed with peers, adolescents, or adults.

➢ Give concrete and specific examples of what is good touch (appropriate affection) and what is bad touch (inappropriate affection) between adults and children.

➢ Model conservative values when asked to participate in questionable or racy activities and assertively say no to unhealthy invitations, whether in the presence of your child or not.

➢ Model safe choices by carrying pepper spray and not walking alone in dark parking lots or other unsafe places.

➢ Teach and role-play with your child how to say a definitive "No!" when they're uncomfortable with a request for participation in an activity or body contact.

➢ Establish clear perimeters as to where the child is allowed to play outdoors.

➢ Make all indoor and outdoor household rules firmly known to the child and all caregivers. Be consistent and stick with the rules without wavering or compromising.

➢ Indoor rules must include boundaries, with right to privacy when the child does not need help using the restroom, bathing, sleeping, dressing, and other similar activities.

➢ Screen all caregivers with background checks.

➢ Teach all family members and caregivers that it is not acceptable to manipulate or force anyone to take part in inappropriate behavior.

➢ Have a simple code word or phrase that your child can say if he feels uncomfortable or unsafe around someone so you can strategically come help him.

➢ Make a list to place on the refrigerator and in all family members' phones with contact information for *trusted adults* the child can call when you aren't around to tell if he feels uncomfortable with someone.

➢ Stipulate very clear guidelines and restrictions on the use of the internet (e.g., no online chat rooms with anonymous people), cell phones, cameras, and social media with peers/adults. Set up a program or app to ban access to pornography. Keep the family computer visible to everyone.

➢ Have a plan of action if a child or adult is violated unexpectedly on the computer with random pornography. If it's a child that stumbles across pornography, teach him to do an immediate about-face and tell a trusted adult right away. If it's an adult, fix the inappropriate content issue on the computer.

➤ Reiterate to the child that he is to command respect by always saying no when he doesn't want body contact or wants privacy, and that it's very important to tell a trusted adult right away about any inappropriate requests made of him. Reassure him that all children and adults in the family will be respected and supported when they say no.

➤ Inform all trusted adults and family about the importance of your child's safety and for everyone to cooperate and follow the Body Safety Family Plan.

➤ All adults and children must speak up if any inappropriate behaviors are observed within their household or other households or in the community.

➤ All observed, suspected, or experienced attempts to sexually abuse must be reported to the authorities immediately.

➤ Have an open-door/phone policy for discussing with other trusted adults and children the problem of sexual abuse and proposed solutions without shame. No questions are too unimportant to ask.

➤ Ensure everyone understands the difference between a good secret, like a surprise, which will soon bring joy, and a bad secret, which is meant to be kept always and when revealed will bring sorrow.

➤ Encourage family members to tell one another about all sexually inappropriate threats or behavior.

➤ Inform family members of any convicted sex offenders that live in your community. Research the sex offender registry at National Sex Offender Registry at www.nsopr.gov before moving into a community.

➤ Develop a Resource List with contact information the child or trusted adults can use to call or go to for help.

A Grandparent's Role in CSA Prevention & Protection

Since studies have shown that most often the perpetrators who abuse children are family, friends, caregivers, or other "trusted" adults, grandparents play an exclusive role in knowing who these trusted others are, as well as in training their grandchildren on body safety. It's common that grandparents have access to knowledge about relatives and friends, which sometimes parents, in the hustle and bustle of work, running a household, and doing life, may overlook.

It may be grievous, but a grandparent has to admit if their own spouse, other grandparent, or relative has been sexually inappropriate toward the child. Having the bravery not to deny who has attempted or can potentially abuse a child gives the grandparent a huge opportunity to identify the risk factors, protect the child, and advocate for the child *before* they are abused.

A grandparent's position, with their voice in the family, increases the chances of preventing someone in the family or extended family from acting out their sexual improprieties. A grandparent can encourage a grandchild to tell immediately if he feels unsafe with anyone's touch. The grandparent's role in addressing any concerns with sexually immoral behaviors can lead to steps taken to protect each child in the family and encourages parents or caregivers to develop a safety plan against CSA.

The secret is out about CSA, and today's grandparents can train themselves to speak up about child sexual abuse in age-appropriate ways amongst their grandchildren and any child who appears to be a target. It is both the biological and forensic responsibility of a grandparent to protect the spiritual, emotional, and physical health of their grandchildren, as well as to prevent CSA from transmitting into the next generation!

If a grandparent refuses to acknowledge the reality of any danger involved, it is the same as a parent's denial; it places the child at risk. A grandparent has received the torch of learning: that life wisdom gives a grandparent the privilege of initiating discussions with grandchildren and all family members in order to encourage direct action against child sexual abuse. A grandparent has earned the authority to gently prod the grandchild to have a voice. And if sexual abuse is suspected, then the grandparent can instruct adult family members to speak up to prevent future abuse and to confront and report the perpetrator.

There are so many possibilities for how a grandparent can help to protect their grandchildren and prevent CSA. Here are a few ways:

- A grandparent usually has knowledge of any history of sexual abuse in the family, and can share that history with the parents and relatives in the immediate family, especially when CSA behaviors have been observed. By doing so, they can prevent further harm to children.

- A grandparent, if trained in CSA prevention or if they have a family history of abuse, is able to recognize the signs and identify the profile of a sexual abuser as well as symptoms of sexual abuse in a child that would otherwise behave normally.

- A grandparent can serve in the role of a trusted adult with a child that needs extra privacy to self-disclose.

- A grandparent can offer a safe sanctuary in the home if a child is fearful of being home alone or in the presence of a perpetrator in their home.

- A grandparent who is separated from the emotional conflict of CSA can offer to listen and guide the child and walk with other family members through the disturbing dynamics of CSA.

- A grandparent may have the flexibility and voice that allows for taking vulnerable risks to speak up on behalf of the family to prevent CSA and protect current and future generations from sexual abuse.

- A grandparent can spiritually supplement and reinforce what a parent or caregiver has taught the child about God's plan for our bodies, and has the privilege to mentor healthy human sexuality from God's perspective.

Child Sexual Abuse (CSA) Symptoms

Below is a list of symptoms to begin your observations and investigation of your child's safety. The presence of these symptoms does not conclusively state that your child has been sexually abused, because several of these can also occur during a child's major life transitions, such as the death of a loved one or divorce. Or, for instance, in many family violence cases, academic challenges are a symptom even when sexual abuse is not involved. Use discretion and discernment in not allowing one symptom—such as depression, for example—to identify the possibility of sexual abuse. In most instances, there are multiple symptoms visible when a child is being sexually abused, and a parent or caregiver is wise to investigate the culprit of those symptoms:

1. The child develops a sleeping disorder, wakes up anxious/frightened, has night terrors, or fears being left alone.

2. The child loses his typical facial affect and appears distant, has unexplainable mood swings, or is clingy.

3. The child regresses into infantile behaviors (wets bed, carries stuffed animal/blanket, sucks thumb).

4. The child refuses to be left alone with anyone else but the parent or caregiver.

5. The child refuses routine removal of clothes for bathing or changing.

6. The child is frightened by certain places for unknown reasons.

7. The child indicates he has a secret with someone, but will not tell anyone.

8. The child begins to talk like an adult and uses sexual language while playing with toys or peers.

9. The child becomes clandestine while using the internet or cell phone.

10. The child suddenly has access to unexplained gifts or money.

11. The child develops headaches, stomachaches, or other physical symptoms, but no illness is found.

12. The child develops an eating disorder (e.g., anorexia or bulimia).

13. The child has multiple unexplainable diaper rashes, yeast or uterine track infections, sores, pain in genital or mouth area, or is diagnosed with an STD or pregnancy.

14. The child self-mutilates (cutting, burning, etc.), uses alcohol or drugs, or runs away.

15. The child becomes angry when God is mentioned.

How to Address CSA with the Offender Privately & in Public

Though it may feel counterintuitive, it is important to maintain composure when dealing with the discovery of CSA. When you feel shock, outrage, anger, hurt feelings, and grief, whether toward the sexual offender, the adult that was supposed to take care of the child, the organization whose watch they were under, or even toward God, if you want to resolve the problems associated with the CSA, what you must instead is display polite calmness. Do not verbally or physically attack the suspected offender. With a cool head, approach the sexual abuser and articulate his offense.

If your child reports improper touch, if you've observed your child being handled by inappropriate touch, or if you simply feel discomfort when you watch the interactions of an adult with your child, this is not a time to wonder if the allegations are baseless or if addressing them will offend. It is not a time to go into fight mode over what may have been done to your child. It is a time to gather all of your explosive anger and use that energy to approach the adult! Not in a mean-spirited way, but with clarity and a zero-tolerance attitude. It is time to address the concern with the person in a purposeful tone of voice and let them know that their behavior is not acceptable.

Easier said than done, you say? You're right. If you don't use the technique of *mindfulness,* making a conscious effort to observe, identify, and acknowledge the state and sensations in your Spirit, Mind, and Body, you will not be able to regain the composure you had before the suspected CSA or before your child was abused. If you are to address the incident in a productive and calm state, you must immediately work to recover an even-tempered Spirit, Mind, and Body.

This effort to restrain your natural human reaction is not about denying or normalizing the incident. It is about acknowledging what has happened, accepting all your feelings, and setting your focus on responding productively, not reacting unproductively. This mindful approach does not mean you don't compute and process the incident. It means that you don't allow your temper to hijack your clear thinking and composed response. Don't go into an ineffective emotional tsunami. If you want effective results to come from addressing the CSA, stay composed.

Mindfulness requires you to self-regulate your focus and your behavior and to redirect it toward a problem-solving response. Taking a mindful approach allows you to return to the current moment in order to stay aware of what's going on presently and address it. Without mindful self-regulation, there is impulsivity. Self-control is usually a characteristic of maturity. It inhibits impulses and is a behavior that can be learned as a part of the socialization process (sometimes utilized unconsciously, because it is a learned action). But self-control does not always last. It is not possible to consciously guide and manage thoughts, feelings, and behaviors without self-regulation.

Self-regulation is a neurological approach. Self-regulation takes place when a person chooses to use their prefrontal cortex. (This is the part of the brain responsible for executive functions, such as reasoning, judgment, emotional regulation, social skills, managing aggression, goal setting, planning, and impulse control.) When you use your pre-frontal cortex to self-regulate, you reduce the intensity and frequency of your impulses to fight or engage in emotional and unproductive behaviors (which stem from the amygdala portion of the brain). The best way to help your child after a CSA-related incident is through self-regulation, or mindfulness.

Self-regulation is not an automatic pilot occurrence; it is a gift from God and an intervention you can teach yourself. Do not attempt to self-regulate or address any CSA situation without God's assistance. He knows all about self-regulation because He designed your brain and its ability to self-regulate. He has also endured any type of suffering thoughts and feelings you can experience. God's Word promises that He is available to be present with you in your time of need. He is a God of love and compassion. He promises to provide you with His mercy and strength when you ask for it. A lot of parents and caregivers react when they discover CSA and approach addressing or reporting CSA with fear and trepidation. They remain in the aftershock mode. There is a calmer and safer approach, and that is to venture into the CSA crisis with certainty by inviting God to go with you.

When you confront the offender, he may try to use his self-believed power to manipulate and intimidate you. He may get defensive, lower his voice, or become hostile and volatile. He may use offensive language or attempt to make threats. But remember, God is the One with the power. He is the Creator of the world, the Maker of you and your child. If you ask, He will go with you to address the offender. God will not allow the offender to overpower you. Won't you invite Him to accompany you? *Have I not commanded you? Be strong and of good courage; do not be afraid, nor be dismayed, for the Lord your God is with you wherever you go* (Joshua 1:9).

The guidelines of addressing a CSA incident follow below. This is a non-exhaustive list of possible scenarios with suggested interventions and responses. As with any safety risk, be certain to address the offender in an inhabited environment or have someone accompany you:

- Do not question what you have observed between the offender and your child or the validity of your child's distress. Trust you and your child's instincts. Children have a right to share their discomfort with body contact, to decline bodily contact, and to report it to their parent or caregiver. Address the offender immediately.

- Never apologize for approaching someone to discuss suspected or perpetrated CSA. Do not worry about offending the alleged offender. Look him in the eyes and confront him in a cool, calm, and collected manner. Do not have too much pride to address the CSA simply because you might be mistaken. This is not a time to worry about loss of face. Taking CSA safety precautions for your child is more important than your pride.

- Be specific in identifying the behavior that makes you uncomfortable. Be direct and state that you do not believe it is necessary or acceptable for your child to be touched in that manner.

- Expect a response when you address the inappropriate touch. *Listen intently* to the offender's response. Does he deny the accusation, blame anyone or anything else for his behavior, or escalate into a defense of twisted facts? Does he attempt to turn the tables by saying that you are the one with improper thoughts. Most offenders incriminate themselves and reveal the truth by their overt defense mechanisms.

- It's very rare that a suspected offender admits to their inappropriate touch, but, on occasion, they will agree and commit to no body contact with the child. Understand that this cooperation is usually not out of conviction of their wrongdoing, but fear of their spouse, family, or job finding out. And keep in mind, there's no guarantee that the offender will not touch your child or another child just because he says he won't.

- Whether it was grooming behaviors that took place or other forms of CSA, be very transparent on the fact that you are informed about CSA and that you are going to have to report him.

- Regardless of how the suspected offender responds to your addressing his improper touch, it's important that you not keep the incident a secret as he would want you to do. A parent or caregiver must be responsible in protecting their child as well as other children that may be at risk. This means contacting other parents and the school, organization, or his place of employment to alert anyone with children of the CSA incident. In most cases, other adults have already been suspicious of the offender but have not addressed the problem. Taking the time to notify other adults and anyone else involved, in addition to your child, will increase the surveillance for all children and give precedence to their safety.

- If you observe anyone interacting inappropriately in body contact or relating sexually with your child, think *clearly* and *thoroughly* about what you will say. You will be able to be more supportive of your child and provide better safety if you remain calm and do not use reactive words or actions. Reacting to the offender or your child only adds to their trauma. If your child comes to you to disclose and identify an offender, praise the child for being courageous and talking to you about it, and thank him for telling you.

We've discussed a lot about addressing CSA with the sex offender and the public. We must also address what to do when the sex offender is a spouse or your child?

The rules for addressing your spouse or your child are the same as with any other offender. The difference is the traumatic impact on you when you make the discovery or when they disclose the truth to you and when you tell them you must report them. It may be one of the hardest things you will do in your life, but it will also be one of the best actions for the good of your spouse or child and other children. You are called not just by the law to report *all* sexual abuse, but God also commands you to do good as well: *But as for you, brethren, do not grow weary in doing good* (2 Thessalonians 3:13).

What you do for your family, other children, people in general, whether it's about CSA or not, is a matter of following His command to love others and to not cease in doing the right thing. Doing His works of kindness, silently sharing the gospel through your actions, and following His callings by doing for others is what He calls you to do. In fact, doing for others is the same as doing for your Master's Kingdom. And Kingdom work will bless you as well as them! So never tire of being responsible in reporting CSA, because what you do for others, you are also doing for the One who called you to obey.

If you suspect or have witnessed boundary violations or signs of abuse with your child or someone else's child, do not focus on the intentions or motives of the offender, but *immediately* and intentionally reiterate and reinforce the specific boundary that was crossed—*even if you're in a public setting*. Describe the behavior that is inappropriate, violates the rules, or is absolutely not acceptable. For example, you go to pick up your child after his sports practice, and when you don't see him, you find him in the locker room with his coach. You say, "It's against policy for anyone to be in any school room alone with a student." Then set the boundary by saying, "You can converse with my child, but you must take your conversation to an area where there are other staff members." Then move on to what you expect: "I am leaving the school building now, so I'll walk out with both of you while you continue your conversation."

After you have walked out of the school building, do not drive away. Sit in your car and have a teaching moment with your child. Review your concern with him about being in the locker room alone with an adult who knew he was breaking the school policy. This conversation must be done in a caring, non-shameful way. You must make him understand that it's not his fault that the coach broke the rule. Although it may be unpleasant for both of you to have this conversation, it must be had, and it will empower your communication with your child.

Do not be apologetic when you ask your child what the coach was talking to him about. Say, "So what was on coach's mind that he kept you after school?" Remind your child that sometimes adults and other kids play tricks on children's minds by appearing to be kind and interested in them. But they can spend time together when they're not alone, and that should be enough. Explain that whenever someone isolates a person to express their kindness or to tell them how special they are or how cool they are in comparison to their peers or parents, they're usually trying to win them over or trick them into doing something wrong. Then review body safety rules with your child by reminding him to tell you if anyone:

✓ Is talking to him about inappropriate subjects (drugs/alcohol, secrets, privates, body touch);

✓ Is asking for his personal information (cell phone number, email, address, family data, social media);

✓ Has attempted to communicate/spend time outside the scope of their role;

✓ Has teacher/coach "pets" or favored classmates;

✓ Has entered when he's undressing, using the toilet or shower in the locker room;

✓ Wants to know his agenda and attend his activities;

✓ Wants to spend time with him alone before or after activities;

✓ Has attempted physical contact with him or others that looks or feels inappropriate.

Parent/Caregiver Prevention Role

Currently, the primary systems responsible for child sexual abuse are Child Protective Services (CPS) and the criminal justice system. Both systems get involved in child sexual abuse cases after the abuse has already been perpetrated. Both systems are concerned with bringing justice rather than *preventing* child sexual abuse. In this role, neither focuses on developing interventions or proposing solutions to reduce child sexual abuse or to *heal* the consequences of CSA trauma. Moreover, since most children's sexual abuse cases are not reported, neither the protection nor justice of children are properly served.

The school system has done well in some states to offer education to preschool and elementary school children on the recognition of abuse and to teach personal safety skills. However, there's very little evidence that such sexual abuse prevention programs actually curtail the occurrence of child sexual abuse. Therefore, this limited CSA awareness education does nothing to decrease the responsibility of the parental or caregiver systems. Truth be told, parents have to get busy!

Notice that I said the adult parental and caregiver systems are to take the responsibility for gaining knowledge about child sexual abuse? The statistics for child sexual abuse speak for themselves—children are vulnerable and can only do so much to protect themselves from child sexual abuse. You can teach your child about CSA, and you are highly encouraged to do so. But at the end of the day, it is your responsibility to protect the child.

Over 40 percent of sexually abused children are six years old or younger. This age group is more accessible and defenseless to victimization. Children can retain information you teach them about body safety, and it works well to keep them safe for the most part. But when children are attacked by adults in authority, they may be overpowered or scared into submission by their abuser, regardless of the prevention skills you've taught them. This is where adults must take the full responsibility to safeguard their children. Children need adult assistance.

Get involved. Train your children. Get involved in the community. Adults and communities must take the lead in CSA prevention. Child sexual abuse can be subtle, even to the keenest eye. It takes a trained parent, caregiver, or professional to recognize a child sexual abuser and the symptoms of a child who has been sexually abused. When parents/caregivers are trained on all aspects of CSA prevention and protection, the child has a better prognosis in avoiding the long-term consequences of child sexual abuse. Studies show that the earlier a child discloses abuse and the sooner it's addressed, the more likely it is that the child will not be victimized again or victimize others in the future.

In addition to parent and caregiver CSA education, we as a society have a collective responsibility to prevent and protect children from sexual abuse. Getting involved means advocating for programs in our communities, regions, and internationally that support children's health, emotional, and physical development. It means initiating the support for public policies that increase CSA safety for children. Parents and caregivers are able to bring awareness to their community's needs so that public education on CSA can be increased and protective implementation can take place wherever risk factors are identified.

All adults, children, and adolescents need to be taught that child sexual abuse is a crime that often causes serious long-term consequences. At the same time, everyone needs to be told that if a child is molested, there is help available and that the abuse is never the child's fault. The goal is that all parents and caregivers lead the way so that children can feel loved, protected, and safe. A child's home and community are where love is to be and abuse is to not. This confirms that the parent/caregiver is refusing to participate in a world that tolerates or condones inappropriate sexual interactions between adults and children.

Sexual offenders rely on others being silent, whether out of fear, reluctance, or being frozen by confusion. But the adult's job is no more than what is being asked of the child—to speak up! All parents and adults must speak up about the sexual abuse of children and form an alliance to help them become aware of a predator's tactics. They must vow to refrain from making their children more vulnerable by staying silent. They must vow to keep children safe.

It starts with each adult taking responsibility for his own friends and family circles to become educated before child sexual abuse happens and to set the limits and boundaries for their children and the predator. It is best to speak up when boundaries are crossed instead of being paralyzed by the predator and regretting that no limits were set, leaving the child accessible to the perpetrator.

The best strategy you will actively use on your Body Safety Family Plan is reducing and making your child's accessibility to sexual abusers extinct. This can only happen with your *intentional* awareness defense. This requires the parent or caregiver to both speak up and speak out transparently about a safety-first approach to all interactions the child has with adults. The educational concepts to be learned include the ability to identify prospective child sexual abusers and monitoring potential places where the child may be at risk for abuse.

The main method of preventing sexual abuse is educating the child, family members, and all those who will come in contact with the child (including professionals). But it is not just about raising awareness with your child's personal relationships. There are also organizations to which the child will be entrusted. It is not out of place for a parent or caregiver to ask about the rules for the adult-child ratio for educational faculty, church staff, childcare providers, youth leaders, healthcare workers, camp counselors, sports teams, etc. Research suggests that perpetrators set up isolated environments to groom children and ultimately abuse them. If the organizations you speak with do not have standard policies against staff being one-on-one with children, it should warn you to find other ways to minimize any opportunity for a predator to approach your child.

Studies have shown that all abuse, including child sexual abuse, does not discriminate on the basis of a perpetrator's age or education level. To expect a sexual abuser to have self-control simply because he is a highly educated provider of professional care is unrealistic. On the contrary, sexual abusers of higher levels of trust use their positions of power to create an air of trustworthiness, and believe they are shielded by their titles and will be trusted with one-on-one time with children.

It doesn't matter if your child has piano lessons or a medical appointment, your presence or the presence of others in the room is necessary for their safety. If you will not be in the room with your child, select a place for them to receive professional services where there are windows that allow you to see into the room either on the doors or external walls. You or another trusted adult's presence are the best protection for your child—not the professional adult that wants alone time with your child.

If you are asked to leave a medical room where your child is being treated, you have the right to request that a staff member or assistant be in the room in place of you. When you enroll your child in school, it is your right to ask about school policies regarding one-on-one time between students and faculty and how the problem of child sexual abuse is managed within their system. It is far from uncommon for children to be abused by adults in organizations that conceal any evidence of child sexual abuse reported in order to protect their organization. This is when parents and caregivers must hold a forum to strategize how to report the organization that is hiding suspected CSA.

If your child is involved in extracurricular activities, your line of defense is a thorough inspection of the adults or youth who will be working with them, along with gathering details on the location and organization itself. As a parent, you must expect child safety to be respected and prioritized. Never compromised simply because someone else approves it. God's and yours are the only approvals that matter. Be sure not to just conduct your preliminary inspection but to periodically show up early to pick up your child to inspect.

Ask the following questions:

A. Does the organization have a seminar or educational program in place that requires all volunteers or employees to be trained in child sexual abuse safety? Does the institution require CSA continuing education for all staff working with the organization?

B. Does the hiring of all staff have a protocol and process that requires background checks? Even though predators often pass lie detector tests, if the organization has a no-tolerance policy, they will insist on contacting former places of employment or volunteer work to verify conduct or any complaints of improper behavior (which most molesters have a history of).

C. Does the institution have a no-tolerance firing policy for inappropriate behaviors with minors?

D. Is the staff provided with resource contact information to make a report should they suspect improper behaviors with a minor?

E. Do the policies and procedures reflect a rule that no adults are to be isolated one-on-one with children?

Whether your child will be spending time with an organization's staff member or with a childcare worker of any kind, it is worth your time and money to conduct substantial interviews, get multiple references, and invest in background checks. Require your childcare provider to take an online course on sexual abuse prevention called "Darkness to Light" (see Resources) as part of their employment agreement.

Childcare is hard work, and just like any employer, a parent should offer an orientation to the child's home and routine. Preferably, the parent should require a couple of days or more of training to make the adjustment for both child and worker smooth. This will also reassure you of whether it's a good match for your child and family.

Occasionally ask your child how the caregiver is working out, and come home for lunch unannounced or arrive home from work earlier than usual to "inspect what you expect." Develop a relationship with the caregiver. Listen to her so that you can get to know her, her friends, and her family. This will reassure you and allow you to learn whether she lives a healthy and balanced lifestyle or if there's any reason for concern.

If you have to travel overnight and you trust your caregiver to watch your child, make sure that you have a quick body safety review/refresher with your child prior to your trip—the same way you would if you were leaving him with relatives or friends. This review is not about hounding or exasperating your child. It's about the fact that in the same way he forgets other rules you've taught him, he may forget parts of your CSA training. House and safety rules should be periodically reviewed at certain stages of their lives anyway, and a responsible parent does not have to apologize for it.

It is your duty to scout out your child's wellbeing. Not in an overprotective, helicopter-parent way, not in a controlling way, but in a gentle, "I love you and care about you" way. With CSA prevention and protection, time is of the essence. It doesn't have to be a deep or frightening discussion, but it can be a way of reassuring your child that you care about his safety and reminding him that you're available if he needs to call you to talk. When you return from out of town, be sure to ask your child in a relaxed way how it went when you were out of town.

Always keep a list of other childcare workers who applied and had excellent references, because if at any point you distrust your current worker, it is better and of utmost importance that you let her go based on an unfounded lack of trust than to take the chance and potentially put your child at risk.

If your child is going to be cared for in the childcare worker's home, it is imperative for you to check out who else lives there and who else will be interacting with him or them. Be clear about household rules and boundaries. You should insist on them having absolutely no visitors while they're providing childcare. Insist that your child have privacy when undressing and using the restroom unless help is needed, and on an open-door policy when your child is alone in any room in the house.

If your child has to stay overnight or on weekends with a childcare worker and is invited to partake in her family's activities, share with your child and the childcare worker that the respect for privacy and body contact is the same for all family members in their household. Instruct them that the rule is for your child to stay in their sight at all times during family gatherings and on outings. Make sure the worker understands the Body Safety Family Plan and has no hesitation about using it.

You also have a right to not hire anyone who has a clean background but whose appearance or actions raise your intuition or make the child feel uncomfortable. The most important part is to execute a body safety plan that will enhance the security of your child and provide autonomy for your child to say no to unnecessary or inappropriate body contact. He should sense and know that his safety and protection are your priority.

Steps to Protect Your Child and Prevent CSA

1. *Learn the facts* about CSA. Child sexual abuse is a problem for grownups to handle. Children are not responsible for warding off sexual advances. Take the grownup responsibility to train your child about CSA body safety to protect your child from sexual abuse.

2. *Eliminate opportunity and access* to your child. Teaching them about stranger danger is helpful, however, strangers are not the primary CSA offenders. The child is at greater risk for CSA from family, friends, and trusted older children and grownups. Abusers are unrecognizable and can go undetected, so take the steps to keep the offender from gaining access to your child.

3. *Believe your child* when he reports discomfort with a peer, older child, or grownup, or when he discloses abuse. The child's trust has been violated. Do not violate his trust of you as well. A child who is molested/assaulted and keeps the abuse a secret or who is not believed is at higher risk for spiritual, mental, and physical trauma that can last a lifetime.

4. *Respond calmly* if your child discloses CSA of himself or a peer. Sometimes a child will gauge the parent's response by pretending the CSA happened to a peer. If a parent reacts negatively, the child usually limits his disclosure or will not disclose further.

5. *Monitor your child's activities* to be certain that he is not easy prey in isolated settings and that several grownups are supervising during activities. Screen carpooler backgrounds, even if they're trusted grownups. Discuss plans before and after activities and watch your child's mood for red flags. In the home, oversee the child's internet/cell phone use.

6. ***Talk about CSA*** safety with your child at an age-appropriate level. Openly notify *all* adults who will be working with them that your child and your family are trained in CSA safety. Yes, it's worth your child's safety to be direct about their protection and your expectation for boundaries. Sometimes a child will tell a trusted grownup before a parent; that is why it's important to talk to all grownups about CSA and the Body Safety Family Plan that's in place.

7. ***Nurture healthy one-on-one mentoring.*** Run background checks/screening even if it's a trusted youth/grownup. Ask for specific details of planned activity and occasionally drop by unexpectedly or arrive early to pick up your child. If your child is receiving lessons/ tutoring in your home and you aren't in the room, supervise sessions with in-home video monitoring systems.

8. ***Teach your child never to give out identifying personal information*** (name, address, email, phone number) in person or over the internet.

9. ***Learn and know the signs of abuse*** and know your child well, because some children do not show any signs or evidence of their CSA. If you know your child's personality and typical behavioral patterns, you will instinctually be aware of suspicious emotional or unbalanced behaviors, such as being more compliant than usual, isolation, despondent moods, and unexplained mood swings anywhere from disrespectful rudeness to a need to be perfect with rules. Any rebellious or atypical misbehavior is a cry for help and is symptomatic of trauma.

10. ***Get help if your child is sexually abused/assaulted.*** Call the *National Children's Alliance* to obtain the location of your nearest *Children's Advocacy Center* to take your child in for a physical exam and psychological evaluation and treatment: **1-800-239-9950; http:// www.nca-online.org.** If there's no center nearby, call **Child Protective Services or other civil authorities** in your area.

11. ***Report your child's or other children's CSA.*** The ability to convict a sex offender is more likely when evidence is obtained from a medical and mental health exam. Include any pornography in the report if used, as it is illegal. For the location and phone number to report CSA in your state, go to the Child Welfare Information Gateway website: **www. childwelfare.gov.**

12. ***Be a responsible grownup and encourage other grownups to be responsible about CSA.*** Initiate and lobby for policies that eliminate one-on-one isolated activities between children, youth, and grownups at *all* children's organizations and places of extracurricular activities. Avoid organizations and programs that are not interested in and do not have a policy against one-on-one time *and* screenings with criminal background checks. If not already in place, recommend for staff to be trained on CSA in the workplace and at children's organizations. Raise conscious awareness about CSA in your community. Support and influence CSA safety. Notify other grownups about sex offenders in the area.

PART III
OVERCOMING CHILD SEXUAL ABUSE

Be merciful to me, O God, be merciful to me! For my soul trusts in You; and in the shadow of Your wings I will make my refuge, until these calamities have passed by.

Psalm 57:1

If Your Child Discloses Sexual Abuse

➢ Believe and protect the child. It's extremely rare for children to fib about being molested.

➢ Calmly tell your child that it's not his fault, that he's not in trouble, and that you are pleased he has done the right thing by telling you about it.

➢ Tell the child that what happened to him is totally the fault of the offender.

➢ Do not berate the offender. Instead, stay neutral in your facial expression and non-verbal language. Stay calm because it will affect your child's willingness to continue to disclose sexual abuse.

➢ Listen to all details the child reports without interrupting, because that is the testimony of evidence. *Tell* your child that you believe him.

➢ If the child has been involved in CSA for some time, reassure him that it's never too late to tell.

➢ Respect your child's privacy. Refrain from disclosing his sexual abuse trauma to anyone that does not need to be informed.

➢ After gathering the child's self-reported facts, confirm that he is not in imminent danger.

➢ If the child was molested, take him to an urgent care clinic to obtain a child wellness exam. Be certain that the child is scheduled for professional help with a counselor or victim's advocate who specializes in sexual abuse.

➢ If the child was sexually assaulted, take him to a hospital emergency room. Ask for your child to be examined by a Sexual Assault Response Team (SART). Schedule professional counseling.

➢ Report your child's molestation or assault to the child abuse hotline (see Resources). If you do not report the incident, you are not doing what you asked your child to do: *always tell and never keep it a secret.* If you don't report it, no one can help. Your report protects your child from further harm and prevents future harm, not only for him but for other potential victims. Your report expresses to your child your love, value, and protection of him.

➢ A child who has been sexually abused may face severe long-term mental health consequences. Seek counseling services with a trained professional who works with child sexual abuse. Therapy, especially at the onset of the abuse, can help alleviate or eliminate some of those consequences. Counseling can expedite healing. It can also intervene on and work to stop the intragenerational and intergenerational transmission of child sexual abuse.

➢ Seek legal assistance from an attorney who specializes in child abuse. Healing is accelerated for your child if he knows you are legally protecting him from the offender. If the judicial system does not provide adequate protection for a child, visit the National Center for Victims of Crime at **www.ncvc.org** or call **1-800-FYI-CALL** for referral information.

If Your Child Is Sexually Assaulted

➢ Stay calm and do not become angry at the abuser.

➢ Do not deny or deflate your child's disclosure. It is very unlikely that your child would make up a story about being traumatized by sexual assault. The loving step to take is not to challenge the child's sharing—*believe your child.*

➢ Do reaffirm your child for his telling you what happened. Reaffirm that what happened to him is the abuser's fault.

➢ Tell your child how sorry you are to hear that he has been attacked in such a hurtful way.

➢ Be patient if your child pauses or cries. Give him time to tell you exactly what happened.

➢ Reassure your child that you are on his side and that you will report the sexual assault and obtain supportive counseling to help him deal with this experience.

➢ Make certain that the child is not in eminent danger, then report the assault using the child's words.

➢ Tell your child you are available 24/7 if he needs to talk again and as often as he needs.

➢ Pray with your child after the assault and maintain a praying bond with him so that each time he turns to you with questions or concerns regarding the assault, you can soothe, encourage, comfort, and provide hope by way of praying with him and for him.

➢ DO NOT clean up your child, even though your loving heart wants to nurture and help him get washed. I know this is painfully difficult not to do, but what your child needs most is to get medical care and for you to allow the authorities all the evidence that they need (which includes your child's clothes and any DNA samples).

➤ Gather a full set of clothes and shoes for your child and take it with you so he can change into it after his medical examination.

➤ Take your child to receive immediate medical care, even if your child appears to have minimal or no physical injury. Be sure to take your child to a medical facility that provides sexual assault services, preferably one with a special child victim's program.

➤ You can find sexual assault medical care for your child by searching the internet, contacting a community rape crisis center, or by calling your local police department or nearest hospital emergency room.

➤ At the medical facility, quietly ask for your child to be examined by someone who specializes in child sexual assault.

➤ Ask the staff to notify your family doctor and send a copy of the examination to him.

➤ Be sure that the police are notified so that your medical visit is documented in a police report (not all medical clinics call the police). A police officer of your child's same gender is best for the sexual assault interview.

➤ Protect your child and do not allow medical or police staff to re-traumatize him by repeatedly questioning him about the sexual assault. Unless your child requires surgical or intensive care and you cannot be there with him, DO NOT leave your child alone, even with trusted medical staff (no matter what they tell you). Make yourself available to stay by your child's side and answer their questions.

➤ Obtain the names and contact information of every police, FBI, or medical staff who works with your child.

➤ Keep reassuring your child that he can count on you to stay by his side and that you will help him get through this traumatic experience.

➤ Reassure yourself through prayer, devotional time, and by sensing His presence through His Holy Spirit, Who tells you that though you and your child may be afflicted today, God will meet you at your place of affliction.

You and Your Child Can Overcome CSA

If your child was not able to escape child sexual abuse/assault, there's no reason he cannot, with God's help, be healed from his trauma. There's no reason why he cannot, with you by his side, be renewed to an *Overcomer's life*. There will be some long days and nights ahead for you, but with an Overcomer's approach, you will be able to calm yourself so that you can best assist them.

Reina Davison

Sometimes after CSA, your child will become anxious or increasingly fearful at bedtime and may not want to go to bed or will want the light to be left on. When this happens, speak gently and calmly to him and offer to tuck him in with prayer and his favorite stuffed animal. Some children find it soothing to listen to a parent softly sing a favorite song, as they did when they were of lullaby age. Reassure your child of God's presence. Soothingly tell him, "No need to fear; God is near. He is right here." If he's a visual child and needs a symbolic comfort, offer to place his Bible next to him on the bed or under his pillow. Teach him that the Bible says God's Word is really God Himself—that God is the Word. "In the beginning was the Word, and the Word was with God, and the Word was God" (John 1:1).

Living with an Overcomer attitude and role modeling that confidence and faith is the *only way* (through Christ) that a human can reach their highest point in life—why wouldn't you want that kind of life for you, your child, and your family? Do not succumb to despondency and an inert and impotent life after CSA. There are so many examples of people in the Bible (too many to cite) who were once in the crisis of their life. They were so disheartened that they were in the mire of despair. But in each and every case, God was present when they turned to Him, and God handled their circumstances according to His Word—as the Creator of the heavens and the earth. Just like the men and women of the Bible, when in crisis, the parent or caretaker must decide to either make the crisis the disaster of their life or to see it as an opportunity for a breakthrough. A chance to do something about the abuser and abuse.

Take a spiritual pause and breathe deeply right now. Breathe in as if you're pulling divine oxygen, transmitted through the Holy Spirit, into your lungs. The CSA circumstances in which you find yourself may feel surreal and severely disturbing, and at some moments you may feel unable to comprehend how this could have happened. Your peace of mind has been totally wrecked. You may even question God's love and presence. Only God didn't hurt your child. He doesn't participate in evil. Was He there when your child was harmed? Yes. So then why, you may be asking, was the perpetrator allowed to hurt your child? The answer is free will and evil.

Both your child and the perpetrator have free will. Free will that can be trained up in God . . . or not. The perpetrator alone is accountable for his evil power and authority over the child and for using his free will as CSA self-entitlement. The innocent child, as has been said, is not to blame for the evil that made use of its free will.

After CSA, or after any crisis, is not a time to question God's love or presence. Doing so exacerbates crisis matters. Instead, it is a time to *rely* on His love and presence. God's wisdom and power far surpass ours. Perhaps we don't understand His Ways, but we have sufficient information on the limitless measure of His love to help us to trust in Him. *For as the heavens are higher than the earth, So are My ways higher than your ways, And My thoughts than your thoughts* (Isaiah 55:9).

God didn't say not to bring your deep questions to Him. In fact, He encouraged us to come to Him with our difficult questions. Often, questioning God increases stress, because when God does not answer the difficult questions, some are led to blame Him for their problems or use Him as an excuse for not doing something about it. God will always act as a righteous God. He is sinless. He never causes the problem. Instead, He can be trusted with our problems because His thoughts and ways are far above our knowledge and understanding. God has all the answers, but He's not required to reveal them because He is God.

God sees the adversity you're going through with His long-range eyes. He can see your life in its entirety—the past, present, and future—and He will accomplish His perfect objective with it. God can, if you believe and trust in Him, rearrange the CSA evil that happened for the benefit of your child and all of those around him. This is how an Overcomer would approach the CSA circumstance: by not questioning God's position on the CSA incident. An Overcomer, by faith, knows God is good and *not* evil. An Overcomer knows that He can, in fact, birth good out of evil. It's similar to what God did when He turned the evil of Golgotha and Christ's crucifixion into a victorious resurrection that brought good to the world!

You have not lost God's benevolence because of CSA. And you are not the only one who has ever questioned His presence. There are others in biblical times and in modern times who have believed God wasn't present. There have been and continue to be victims of CSA and other types of abuse who wonder where God was when they were suffering. Even Job, a devout and faithful man of God, said when undergoing his crisis: *Oh, that I were as in months past, As in the days when God watched over me; when His lamp shone upon my head, and when by His light I walked through darkness; just as I was in the days of my prime, when the friendly counsel of God was over my tent; when the Almighty was yet with me* (Job 29:2-5). Can you imagine, after reading that, the isolation and abandonment Job must have felt?

People occasionally lose their spiritual way. Maybe it's because they've ignored God and not spent time with Him and in His Word. Or maybe they've been actively engaging against God's principles. This can easily happen to someone who's facing what seems an insurmountable crisis. However, it is in those dark crisis circumstances that we need to hold on to our faith, just as Job did, in spite of his despair. It is now, especially, that we need to place our belief and trust in Christ, Who is God's presence and Who has promised never to abandon His people. Do as Job did after his discourse: in faith, think of the goodness of God, and remind yourself frequently how He has directed your path thus far.

Think about how He has protected you, your child, and your family in the past after a crisis. Christ does not change in His love or in His presence. As He has done in your past crises, He will do again. He is waiting for you to turn to Him with all of your hardships. Go ahead—lay all of them down before Him. True to His Word and promises, God's perfect love will vanquish *all fear*. You will be enveloped in His Arms of love, just as soon as you reach out to Him.

There are a few hazards which can have potentially traumatic effects on the Spirit, Mind, and Body. CSA is one of those. Such hazards influence the person's subconscious to a degree that their mental abilities become impaired. In some cases, this lack of clarity creates lifelong consequences.

When Jesus walked the earth and He called all those who were weary and burdened over to Him, He didn't provide a warranty that would exempt them from life problems, and He didn't promise that they would be trouble-free evermore. Instead, He asked for them to share their burden with Him and offered to teach them how to cope so that they could be set free from their crises—and experience His peace.

No one can predict life's setbacks. No one can foresee or measure how traumatic future incidents will be. But the wisdom we can learn from His Word prepares us to handle crises when they occur.

To doubt that in this life we will have troubles is to be unprepared for eventualities, and this belief can have destructive results. In order to live a balanced life of Spirit, Mind, and Body that is prepared for crises, one must have a healthy, connected, personal relationship with Christ. As an Overcomer, remain near to God's presence through fervent prayer, contemplation, praise, thankfulness, and supplication. An Overcomer who does this finds that when a crisis strikes, Christ's presence will be felt, and He will be there to help them triumph over the crisis with a heart full of His peace. There is truth in James 4:8: *Draw near to God, and He will draw near to you.*

The depth, growth, and commitment of your spiritual walk with God are your responsibility. You could plead with God to draw nearer to you and to develop your faith, but if you don't activate and exercise the level of faith you currently have, you cannot expect God to increase it. For instance, no matter how much you desire a deeper prayer life, only *you* can sit silent and still, waiting patiently on God to reveal His holy presence. And only *you* can sense and become aware of His Being.

God has already planted a yearning for Him in all of His people. Some are just not aware that the void they feel is their need for God. The yearning God has planted must be cultivated in one's deepest self. This desire to get to know Him is empowered by the Holy Spirit and is one of His greatest gifts to you. He calls on you through His Spirit to answer your yearning for Him. He has a gift for you—the gift of Christ.

God's Word says that He calls out, *Come to Me,* but it is our total responsibility to answer. Our answer will determine the level of our commitment in pursuing a close relationship with Him. To fulfill your responsibility to Christ as an Overcomer is a solemn undertaking. If you hesitantly or half-heartedly accept Christ, God will know it, and you will deprive yourself of a true relationship with Him.

God's offer of communion with Him is for your entire life span. If you only offer a lackluster relationship to God, you will live in the pits of an ailing faith. God requires that you surrender your life in the world in exchange for a devoted, divine life with Him. He would never take away something in your life without replacing it with something better.

The life you're currently living is a temporary life. The life He's offering you is evermore. It is eternal. By accepting responsibility for your own spiritual development, you will continually grow closer and closer to your Redeemer.

When your child is sexually abused or assaulted, you will need every ounce of your faith and strength to recharge your Overcomer, Christ-centered perspective: *We are hard-pressed on every side, yet not crushed; we are perplexed, but not in despair; persecuted, but not forsaken; struck down, but not destroyed—always carrying about in the body the dying of the Lord Jesus, that the life of Jesus also may be manifested in our body* (2 Corinthians 4:8-10). When the crisis of CSA hits your household and you're in the midst of that excruciating anguish, remember to Whom you and your child belong . . . you are both linked to Christ. And because of that connection, you *can* overcome this crisis!

An Overcomer does not submit to the world's way of engaging in or passively enabling CSA. An Overcomer does not surrender to the evils of child sexual abuse and assault. Overcomers have a much greater purpose than to allow CSA to make them a victim. They have a purpose beyond living in the bondage of trauma as if they were on house arrest. If CSA visits your life, you turn to the One Who loves you, the only One Who matters, and the One Who will see you and your child through this passing crisis.

I do not mean to minimize your family's suffering by calling it a passing crisis. To call it that is not the same as saying "this too shall pass." I know you and your child are deeply hurt on every level, and the last thing I would want to do is downplay what has happened. But what I offer for your review is the fact that the trauma of CSA is greater and more difficult to heal from for victims who yield to it.

Caving in and falling ill with the symptoms of CSA results in never-ending despair. And the act of just barely surviving results in being pulled down by the unresolved trauma. *Doing* something to overcome the crisis provides catharsis. It alleviates the symptoms and results in permanent relief (everlasting peace).

Notice that I previously used the phrase "if CSA *visits* your life," and that I use the word "crisis" to refer to the experience and aftermath of CSA. I chose these two words intentionally, because a *visit* is for a short time or season, and a *crisis* is a stage and also for a season. It is up to you whether it will be a permanent trend or a turning point for all future events.

Some parents/caregivers perceive the CSA trauma as a time of unmendable hurt and an "irreparable damage," as some CSA professionals would say. But from an Overcomer's perspective, it is indeed viewed as a turning point. An opportunity to move forward with a refreshed perspective and a more productive direction. As one Overcomer parent put it to me after she discovered her spouse had abused their daughter, *I am moving forward with new knowledge. I guess I was naïve and never even considered, never even fathomed, that CSA could happen in our marriage. In our very own happy family.*

A CSA crisis or any other crisis can develop opportunities that one could've never had if things had remained the same. A crisis presents an opportunity to have a more in-depth intimate encounter with the risen Christ as you become aware on a higher level that He is alive and ready, 24/7/365, to be there for you in your crisis. Whether you see the crisis as an entrance into the devil's dungeon or as a "Christ, light the way" turning point really depends on your status with Him. You determine your status—not Him. Whether you choose to meet with Him or not is up to you.

This is a momentous decision, because how you respond to the crisis and to Christ will impact how you will pass through the crisis—in light or in darkness. He sees you in your crisis and is gently calling out to you, *Come to Me, all you who labor and are heavy laden, and I will give you rest. Take My yoke upon you and learn from Me, for I am gentle and lowly in heart, and you will find rest for your souls. For My yoke is easy and My burden is light* (Matthew 11:28-30). Will you come to Him or not?

Christ—not the crisis—is the most critical decision in your entire life. You have to choose to either accept or reject His invitation. As a *victim* of CSA, you need to think about this decision. As an Overcomer, there is nothing to think about. You take the opportunity and choose to believe in Him. You entrust your CSA crisis and life to Him. You decide to worship Him alone and to obey His precepts and guidance, during the crisis and evermore.

An Overcomer who accepts the invitation not only releases his/her crisis burden to Christ, but begins to walk in His light and sees more and more of His light everywhere. This crisis becomes the golden opportunity of a lifetime instead of an endless regret—regret over rejecting the abundant life that is offered through Christ.

You can look at the CSA as a temporary evil that needs Christ and mental health treatment to overcome, or you can see it as a lifetime tragedy that can only be band-aided with survival skills. Allow the Lord to handle your crisis. Don't serve the crisis—serve Him by giving Him the honor to help you manage as an Overcomer. An Overcomer's response to the crisis of CSA is the same as Joshua's when he said, *But as for me and my house, we will serve the Lord* (Joshua 24:15).

Through centuries past, victims have had to deal with pain and trials of all forms of abuse, including CSA. But it has always been those Overcomers with a strong, unshakeable belief and firm trust in Christ that were able to withstand, overcome, and be victorious over the abuse. Whatever type of abuse you've experienced, God remains with you to support you and to carry you through its darkness. He has been with victims and Overcomers all along, holding their hands since biblical times: *Fear not, for I am with you; Be not dismayed, for I am your God. I will strengthen you, Yes, I will help you, I will uphold you with My righteous right hand* (Isaiah 41:10). Keep your hand firmly clasped in His!

He is still our God of the Universe. We should exalt Him even when tragedy hits our innermost being. Our response to unbearable crises in our soul still needs to be awe of God's glory and majesty. Even the psalmist whose soul was weary with sorrow turned to God in praise and worship, crying out, *Your testimonies also are my delight and my counselors* (Psalm 119:24). The psalmist goes on to ask God to revive and strengthen him according to His Word (Psalm 119:25, 28). It is when you turn your sorrow over to God and seek His strength that you will find renewal in your spirit. You will find a peace and a hope that He will handle your situation—through His utmost holy and highest power!

The same God Who created the earth and handed out the Ten Commandments, the God Who shared His Word with us and offers His unconditional love and presence in our lives to eternally guide us, this same ever-present God and His Son—the living Christ—can deal with the devastation and trauma of child sexual assault. Though initially a victim's path may be narrow after CSA, Christ, His Word, and His power open up the Spirit, Mind, and Body to deeper and wider horizons for a purposeful life.

God is the divine ruler of the Universe. He reigns over everything that happens in our world because He is its Creator. He is eternally powerful and reigns over all circumstances. He is sovereign—that means He is supreme and has authority over all. The word sovereign even has the word *reign* right in it! In His sovereignty, God can eradicate the trauma of CSA.

Though the earth is ever-changing, God is *unchanging*. He is to be the steadfast Guidance of our lives, not our circumstances. Our circumstances in a world that will one day pass away. God has authority over your family's CSA circumstances. He has the power to help you and your child to overcome child sexual abuse. Won't you allow Him to help you and your child overcome CSA today?

Encourage Your Child

Teach your child that he does not have to perform in order to be loved by God or anyone else in this world. Tell him that it's okay to turn to God with any worries, because there are no worries God can't fix! At the same time, train him on the reality that God does not always answer our prayers in the way that we wish He would. Let your child know that, just like with earthly parents, our heavenly Father gives the best answer to our worries. Reassure your child that he doesn't need to rely on his own limited human strength. He should turn to Jesus in prayer for His super-power strength.

Explain the Trinity to your child and how God, the Son, and the Holy Spirit are all three in One. Remind your child that the Creator has gifted the world with the Holy Spirit, if we accept Him, to lead and guide us as a Helper and Comforter (John 14:26). Tell him that the Holy Spirit living in his heart is not a spooky thing; that it is a supernatural power which he has within him. Your child will be encouraged, knowing that he has that extra edge of God's presence within him to protect and empower him to make safe choices. Teach your child that God is a good, good Father. For some children whose trust has been violated by a male abuser, it becomes difficult to trust that God does love and care about them and that He is good. Read Psalm 119:68 to your child to remind him that God is good and *does* good!

Tell your child that one of the greatest gifts and influences in his life *is* the Holy Spirit, and that he has access to that gift 24/7/365. Reiterate that the Holy Spirit's purpose is to cause the character of Christ to live in him. Speak to him about God's love. Teach him that it is the Holy Spirit's power within him that gives him the love of God to be shared, the same way God shares His love with us. Let him know that the Holy Spirit is available if he feels worried about something. He can pray about it, and the Holy Spirit will help him to calm down and be at peace.

Tell him that if he ever wrestles with temptation and does not know whether something is right or wrong to pray to God, because the Holy Spirit can help him make a decision. Say to him that if he ever feels sad or discouraged, the Holy Spirit will uplift him if he prays and asks God to restore his joy and encouragement. Encourage your child by providing the good news that every good thought that he has is from the Holy Spirit.

Let him know that every good thing that he does is also the Holy Spirit working in him to do good, and that every time he overcomes a doubt or fear through faith in God, the Holy Spirit has been there to support and take care of his uneasiness. Set your child's mind at rest. Reinforce that when he cries out to God, the Holy Spirit is there right away, ready to help, because God's Holy Spirit always moves instantly with compassion.

Hug your child and spur him on to understand with confidence that the Holy Spirit will make him like Christ. That He will lead him away from evil and into Christ's holiness. Make sure your child knows that he doesn't have to do anything extraordinary or out of the ordinary to receive the Holy Spirit—just pray after he asks Jesus into his heart (the prayer of salvation) and ask God to grant him the gift of His Holy Spirit.

Be confident in your child's ability to learn ideas and concepts he has never heard before. This learning is also manifested through the power of the Holy Spirit, even if he doesn't fully comprehend all of your teachings at once. With passing months and years, his growth and understanding will be revealed in his emotional and spiritual maturity. The Holy Spirit is the true foundation for growth in faith and life, for both you and your child. As your child grows intellectually, he will also grow spiritually, as you and other mentors teach him. Your child will become increasingly dynamic and filled with vitality. He will grow in his own personality and you will see that Christ has become a living reality in his life. Christ's love and character will radiate from his heart and life.

Be open for new growth possibilities in your child's life. When God is at work, His actions won't always be predictable, and the plan for your child's life won't always be clear. God has always been original, from the beginning of time. Just look at all the various species He designed and their different roles and purposes—not one is 100 percent like another. Because of God's originality, He breaks into our circumstances with new ideas and creations, new vocabulary, small and big miracles, new instructions or direction—He is full of surprises! He works with His people and He will work with your child, pointing him in new ways that will lead to the destination He has for him. All of these surprises are not surprises to God. They are a part of His sovereign Will and plan. They are a part of His glorious possibilities for your child's life!

Most of the time, God works in mysterious ways that His people never expected. Sometimes His people miss the surprises and blessings by sticking to what they already know and choosing their own will instead of God's. Nevertheless, people are able to look back at some of those surprises, missed or not, and at times recognize them immediately as acts of God.

Teach your child to be mindful and aware of his surroundings and his life as it unfolds. Teach him to look for new things God is busy working on in his life. Tell him that God does not always reveal everything and to look forward to the fun surprises He may have ahead for him. *Behold, I will do a new thing, now it shall spring forth; shall you not know it?* (Isaiah 43:19).

In the meantime, as you watch your child learn from your body safety training and as you bask in the results of your loving protection over him (whether he has or hasn't ever experienced unsafe touch), your child will thrive. And witnessing the fruits of your training and his abuse-free life is only half of the promising journey!

Encourage Yourself

Parents and caregivers are uplifted when they sense accomplishment in teaching their child to make righteous choices. It's worthy to note, nevertheless, that the work of a parent is never done, regardless of a son's or daughter's ages. Prayer is indispensable in raising children in a world that puts them at risk for CSA and other avenues of harm's way. As they age and leave home, they will carry the free will we are all born with. The possibility of satan's temptation and darkness always lies in wait; his DNA is in every dark work any of us chooses.

satan roams and wants to steal your peace. However, God is ever-present and powerful, and He wants you to remain at peace if ever your child turns away from Him. He wants you to pray and to live your life in His amazing grace. He wants you to let *Him* take care of your child's choices.

In other words, no matter how much blood, sweat, and tears a parent pours into the training of a child, the child can depart from his training and choose not to follow God's way. Be encouraged by reminding yourself that God only holds you accountable for your choices and behaviors. Your children, no matter what age, are accountable to Him for themselves. God does not support the sin of CSA. It is against His righteousness, holiness, and will for your child. But since Christ does not force Himself or His ways on anyone, sin is always an option. Each of us must make our own choices. When your children are grown and gone, the best you can do is pray that they continue to choose Him and His ways.

There is always hope that a prodigal son will return. If you trained him in God's righteous ways and you continue to pray for him, there is hope he will return. Sometimes you may not feel like praying for your child or for anyone or anything at all. That's when you need to ask for supernatural strength to pray. Prayer is vital for your child, yourself, and others. Your spiritual prayer mood runs through your veins, and it can either make or break your day. So what's your spiritual pulse today?

If you, as a parent or caregiver, have a history of sexual abuse trauma, pray about that as well. But this is *not* one of those things that's useful to share with your child. When a parent is transparent about their trauma, the child is subjected to secondary traumatic stress just by listening and envisioning their parent being hurt. Purging the trauma and receiving support in a group which specializes in abuse is therapeutic, but disclosing to your child is not.

Seek counseling for yourself instead. Pray and be encouraged into the path of healing. Supplementing individual or group counseling with self-care is very effective in *overcoming* any type of abuse. There are numerous self-care apps to choose from on the internet, some of which can be downloaded to your phone for free or have a minimal annual fee. A self-care app is a good resource to use as an accountability life coach to guide and support you in your goals to live a curated, healthy, de-stressed Overcomer life.

Keep in mind that no matter how long it has been since your own personal trauma with CSA (especially if you're dealing with the added burden of your child's CSA), *Jesus Christ is the same yesterday, today, and forever* (Hebrews 13:8). Christ has acted justly toward His people throughout biblical times—He can be trusted to do the same in modern times. As a part of you and your child's recovery, even if you are at your lowest ebb in life, remember to hide in your heart what Jesus has taught and promised you: *With God all things are possible* (Matthew 19:26). Ask Christ to remove you from the emotional seesaw of CSA. Ask Him to give you the long-term vision and steadfast posture that comes from hiding His Word in your heart.

And while you are doing some self-care, how about encouraging another parent or caregiver from your CSA trusted adults or from your support group to do some self-care for his or herself? How about sharing the principles of becoming an Overcomer of CSA? Don't assume that all CSA victims or CSA victim parents and caregivers know Christ and the Overcomer principles for dealing with CSA. Share your self-care skills *and* your Overcomer, Christ-centered principles. There's a high probability that many of them don't know Christ. There are over seven billion humans on earth. Approximately two billion are Christians. About one billion have heard about Christ but have not accepted Him. *Half* of the world's population reports that they've never heard of Christ. The work the disciples began in biblical times has much more left to be done!

Overcomers need to get to work! No matter how awkward or challenging it may seem to share the Christ-centered principles of an Overcomer, you can ask prayerfully for the strength, the words, and the *power* to share with a fellow CSA parent or caregiver. The Holy Spirit will assist you—if you ask. God taught, trained, instructed, guided, and blessed the disciples in sharing about Christ. He offers to do the same for you.

Unfortunately, with some victims of CSA, perspective is temporarily unclear. The vision of Christ's ability to assist and bless becomes clouded in the midst of the trauma of abuse. As a victim of CSA, you may think you're experiencing a trauma with your child that's unique to our modern world. In a way, that's a valid thought. It certainly feels that way. However, the foundational problems historically and up to the present are the same as in biblical times. The men and women of biblical times suffered from self-centeredness, lust, hatred, immorality, murder, and other conduct disorders that remain today as powerful, sinful influences. If Christ could manage the world's problems in biblical times, He can empower you to Overcome CSA and then to go forward to teach others what you know.

God gave power to the disciples to cover the earth with the good news of Christ. God can do the same for you as you pay it forward to CSA parents and caregivers, to those in your family, your friends, and all throughout the earth! *But you shall receive power when the Holy Spirit has come upon you; and you shall be witnesses to Me in Jerusalem, and in all Judea and Samaria, and to the end of the earth* (Acts 1:8).

To become an Overcomer like Christ is a mission. The Overcomer's mission can never be completed if it is left all up to the missionaries—there are just too many unsaved souls! Each of us must be effective as witnesses for Christ and His Overcomer's mission! Even if you're not excited about Christ's Overcomer mission at the moment, you will know when He is calling you to touch someone's life with the good news of Christ.

You will know it's time to share the gospel, in the exact way the disciples knew that Christ had called them. You will know when you feel compelled to share what Christ has done for you and your child, just like the two friends who walked on the road to Emmaus (Luke 24). Jesus touched their lives, and they were forever changed. He made them Overcomer's simply by showing up in the middle of their sorrow, disappointment, and disillusionment. And when He did, His power was able to reignite their hearts. The scriptures say their hearts burned within them when Christ appeared to them on the road and shared the gospel.

Before Christ showed up, their minds were clouded with confusion and by broken spirits, but Christ soothed their broken hearts and enlightened their thinking. Christ's conversation and questions redirected their thoughts to what really matters. The outpouring of His love overwhelmed them and set their hearts on fire for the gospel of Christ. They hurried back from their journey to share the good news with everyone.

When Christ touches people's hearts, He awakens all their senses. He awakens what was dormant before their encounter with Him. His presence touches a person's heart like no other experience in their life. Their heart is renewed and is now filled with a passion of divine love and conviction. Christ restores energy that had been lost and recovers a person's soul with a spiritual motivation for life like never before.

An Overcomer understands the depth and length of Christ's love, and it's natural for the Overcomer to love Him back. The more an Overcomer loves Christ, the more intimately they will live with Him in their heart. This enables Christ to speak into their life through the Holy Spirit's power. Just like the two friends walking on the road to Emmaus, an Overcomer's heart becomes ignited with His love, and that love, which cannot be contained, reaches out to other prospective Overcomers.

There is Healing and Hope After CSA

Your healing from the trauma of CSA—whether from your child's victimization or both of yours—requires faith in God.

CSA can bring darkness into a person's life. It can devastate and attempt to extinguish any light a person had prior to CSA. It can attempt to steal any vibrancy, hope, and joy that exists in a person's heart. Faith in God restores hope, joy, and recovers a pre-CSA life . . . or better! In times of crisis, when a CSA victim feels all hope is dead, anxiety (the primary symptom of CSA) plants a seed in their Spirit, Mind, and Body. And it grows.

Anxiety is the root and product of low faith and a confused mind. Overcoming anxiety requires the Overcomer to search for and gain insight into the reason(s) or cause of the anxiety. For victims who do not practice mindfulness, their anxiety is just a feeling. They get bogged down with it. Their anxiety is unclear, indescribable, and indefinable, but it continues to wear away and deteriorate their Spirit, Mind, and Body. The victim becomes a slave to the anxiety. The only solution that harvests healthy results is to take the anxieties to God and ask Him to be the Master Physician over the anxiety. When an Overcomer does this, they remove the devil's permission to attack their peaceful approach to present and future crises!

Even with God's help, healing from anxiety is a process. Anxiety requires the development of the fruit of patience. For most CSA victims, not slowing down to process is a main cause of their growing anxiety. So one of the first steps to managing anxiety is to slow down so that you can mindfully acknowledge your symptoms. Once you recognize that you're experiencing anxiety, you can gradually adjust your composure to your pre-anxiety state. Some helpful tools to do this are breathing exercises, positive affirmations, positive self-talk, inspirational reading and music, resting, or removing yourself from anything that amplifies your anxiety.

Anxiety is not something you can just ignore. If you do, it will only increase, and eventually result in a higher level of symptoms. Anxiety has to be recognized and experienced if recovery and healing are to take place. To overcome anxiety, an Overcomer cannot rush through recovery. But they can still recover from their symptoms quickly by working through the process. The sooner the symptoms are accepted, the sooner the Spirit, Mind, and Body can make the healthy adjustment and regain composure.

The primary peril of anxiety is refusing to work on it. It's cozier to stay in the comfort zone of the idea that nothing can be done. It's easier to live with the symptoms . . . at least for a time. However, this only exacerbates the symptoms, eventually creating low confidence, isolation, irritability, low energy, apathy, and depressed moods. In addition, the Spiritual outlook becomes neutral or despondent. Constricted breathing increases, along with tightness of the muscles and connecting tissues.

When anxiety takes place, it's important not to stop taking care of the Spirit, Mind, and Body. All healthy habits must be maintained in order to counteract symptoms. If you have an already established inspirational quiet time, do not quit having your prayer time. If you work out or have a relaxing body routine, do not stop your daily regimen. If you interrupt your healthy daily habits (like exercise, nutritious eating, sufficient sleep) because of anxiety, your anxiety will increase and your ability to problem-solve through your crisis will go downhill. Sure, you may want to adjust your routine by changing things up a bit in order to slow down, but completely shutting down self-care activities will not help reduce symptoms of anxiety.

Anxiety is your enemy! When facing your enemy, a technique I sometimes suggest in order to increase patience in dealing with and managing anxiety is to use one of the U.S. Navy SEAL's mantras: *Slow is Smooth, Smooth is Fast.* It's similar to the U.S. Army's mantras when firing a weapon, dealing with a challenge or the enemy, *Slow is Steady, Steady is Smooth, Smooth is Fast,* and *Crawl, Walk, Run.*

- SLOW down—Deliberately acknowledge the symptoms. Gradually identify the cause of the anxiety. Don't rush through the process.

- SMOOTH—Become as a calm sea. Be flexible with your daily routine, but never give up healthy habits. Learn new adaptation skills. Adjust with new coping strategies.

- FAST—Incorporate all new coping skills, integrate new anxiety management habits, and quickly apply the anxiety reducing methods whenever (if ever) anxiety returns.

Slow and smooth are a matter of developing muscle memory (mindfulness) involving a non-physical automatic response; fast involves physical action. This technique trains your mind to go from slow speed to high-level performance.

Anxiety can flood the Mind and paralyze the Spirit and Body. The Overcomer's strategy then is to slow down (not stop) and gradually ease into coping behaviors that will help him/her to move forward with the calming, high-speed action and peace of God!

Faith is lifted and renewed when anxiety is reduced and overcome. Faith in the Father, Christ, and the Holy Spirit renders a better life because a life lived with faith in God is a life well-lived. It is not a superficial, shallow, self-willed life. It is carefree and deeply rooted in His quiet stillness. It is a stillness that can only be experienced through slowing down and experiencing

His peace—away from the screeching shrill of the realities of CSA. This stillness brings on a life filled with inner joy. It is a life that is full of mindful confidence, born from the stillness, faith, and wisdom that *God* is the Commander-in-Chief of this world.

God is omnipotent over all human and evil forces. He's not only in control of this world, but He has offered the world to us on a silver platter so that in it we might live a life of light and not darkness. An abundant life. *Then Jesus spoke to them again, saying, "I am the light of the world. He who follows Me shall not walk in darkness, but have the light of life"* (John 8:12). It's not possible to experience the fullness of life as He has promised without faith in Him. *I have come that they may have life, and that they may have it more abundantly* (John 10:10). It is still possible after CSA to live a life filled with His love, light, hope, and unending joy. Not as the self-willed world lives, but a life of true, redemptive joy. This, of course, is only possible if an Overcomer has asked Christ to bring His light over the dark areas of theirs and/or their child's life.

Sometimes victims of CSA remain in darkness because they've accepted the fear and confusion and false teachings about CSA, often believing these things will bring good to the child and family. Instead of believing CSA myths, allow Christ to bring light into the darkness of CSA by making Him leader of your family. Submit to His plan for your child's life and all of your loved ones.

God, Christ, and the Holy Spirit are bigger than CSA! Christ owns the world and all of its troubles. He can separate the darkness from the light because He *is* light. *As long as I am in the world, I am the light of the world* (John 9:5). Ask Him in prayer to be your family's light of peace and comfort. When Christ shows up, He shows out! Once you have asked, you will receive. *And whatever things you ask in prayer, believing, you will receive* (Matthew 21:22).

The new beam of light after CSA will stay lit and shine in your child's and family's life. This bright light will illuminate your paths, clearing away CSA trauma. Your Overcomer thoughts will be enlightened and will guide your footsteps to focus on Christ's love and principles. So turn His Light switch on and allow it to live in your Spirit, Mind, and Body!

When an Overcomer accepts God's light of peace and comfort, it means a true harmonious relationship with Christ exists. The Overcomer allows the Holy Spirt of Christ to do spiritual work in their life, so becoming an Overcomer never feels like an inconvenient burden but instead like a joyful gift of life.

Some victims of CSA, whether in personal or secondary trauma, live in denial, suppressing the hurt. But it still lives in blocked memory and comes out in the way their lives are lived. They are imprisoned, and they take those that have been affected by the CSA (the child, family, and others) to prison with them. They live incarcerated by their dark attitudes. They allow CSA to command their lives. Some adolescent/young adult victims respond rather than react to the burden of CSA. They appear to respond with a naïve charm, while older victims may react with self-reproach.

An Overcomer realizes they have been created in the Image of God and are therefore priceless to Him. Because an Overcomer is one with the Father, they can be filled with the self-confidence from the peace God offers and learn to live in harmony with the self. With this inspirational mindfulness, faith, joy, and spiritual peace, the victim can respond to the new life after CSA with faith, supernatural strength, the wisdom of Christ, and the presence of His Holy Spirit. He freely gives you the Holy Spirit to help you deal with all of life—even CSA. Take the life He has generously given you. After all, our lives—victims' and all others—are the reason He came down from heaven and into this world! He came specifically to save us!

Don't sit around and wait for someone or something to take care of the consequences of CSA. If you do not take care of the CSA problem, it won't take care of itself. Some victims of CSA wait to report the incident(s) or to get counseling. Do not wait for the light to be green—it is green when child sexual abuse happens—GO!

Victims often get stuck in a rut of not telling or not reporting, just like the sick man who laid beside the pool at Bethesda for thirty-eight years *doing nothing but waiting* for someone to come along and help him (John 5).The man believed he needed a helping hand in order to make a change. But Christ surprised him when He told him to get up, pick up his mat, and walk! Sure, Christ was still loving in His approach when He commanded him to get up and walk, but He was also direct and firm! His approach challenged the man not to be dependent on others to take care of his illness. It introduced the man to the idea of *doing something* about his sickness. It motivated the man to leave his daily comfort rut of fear and self-pity. It motivated him to stop waiting!

Christ's direction gave him the energy to move forward instead of staying isolated. A better life was ahead for him, but he couldn't experience it until he considered the possibility of walking. When a victim sits on the CSA reporting and treatment, it gnaws at their faith and trust in both themselves and God. This sitting around and taking no action to protect the child and other children against CSA eventually makes them feel like a failure. They feel like a failure because the CSA is in charge of their life. The past controls their present and future. But just like with the sick man at the pool, it doesn't have to stay that way. Christ does not want anyone, child or adult, to wallow by a pool, sick from CSA, a single day longer! He wants you to believe in Him and to swim out of the dark murky waters of CSA and into the light of His living water. *He who believes in Me, as the Scripture has said, out of his heart will flow rivers of living water* (John 7:38).

Revelation 7:17 promises that at the end of time, when Christ returns to earth, He will lead His people to living fountains of water and wipe away every tear. Christ is a God of mercy and compassion; do you think He wants to *wait* until you get to heaven to wipe away your tears? No. God's love is too profound to watch you shed tears and leave you comfortless. He wants to comfort you and wipe away your tears right now.

No matter how long you or your child have been battling the symptoms and consequences of CSA, you don't have to remain emotionally paralyzed anymore. You can stand up today and declare that you will do something about the CSA. You can declare that you are choosing to leave the past behind you! Christ will give you the strength, just like He did for the man at the pool. He will reinstate your trust, and He will be with you from the beginning and all throughout your new journey as an Overcomer.

The health and wholeness of a broken victim of CSA is in God's plan. When CSA happens, God can thwart all future evil plans. When you ask God to take over the CSA trauma with His Authority, He will show His power over evil, and it will open a way for His light, healing, and restoration. All that is needed is for you to take immediate action today!

Because of the extent of Christ's love for the victim and all His people, there are no limits to the abundant life He has prepared for the Overcomer of CSA. Christ's desire is *that Christ may dwell in your hearts through faith; that you, being rooted and grounded in love, may be able to comprehend with all the saints what is the width and length and depth and height—to know the love of Christ which passes knowledge; that you may be filled with all the fullness of God* (Ephesians 3:17-19). As an Overcomer, you and your child's healing does not begin by waiting. It can begin the day that CSA happens. It begins the moment you decide to stand up against CSA, take up your mat, and walk!

If after a CSA incident you were in my office, we would certainly take care of all the evaluations, legal requirements, and reporting (administrative protocols). But I would not allow you and your child to leave without a sense of encouragement and a hope. There is hope after CSA, even if the statistics on unrecovered CSA "survivors" are inordinately large. Life does not have to become an uphill crisis filled with struggle after CSA. There is hope, no matter what the statistics say.

There is hope, even if a "survivor" has experienced the consequences of CSA (physical pain; genital/groin tears, somatic symptoms, insomnia, loss of appetite, eating disorder, headaches, psychological distress/disorder, PTSD) nearly their entire life. *Now hope does not disappoint, because the love of God has been poured out in our hearts by the Holy Spirit who was given to us* (Romans 5:5).

Christ, through the power of the Holy Spirit, can convert you and your child's life from victim to Overcomer. He can transform and transport your life of pain and struggle into one of peace. I encourage both you and your child to consider starting or returning to therapy. If you were in my office today, our conversation would include therapeutic interventions to treat the trauma, but, in addition, my work with you would include the permanent healing and hope that an Overcomer can obtain for a lifetime. We would actively work toward no longer focusing on fear. We would work to stop fear from building up symptoms of PTSD. We would work on eliminating those haunting thoughts of the CSA incident and of "what could have been." We would work to eliminate the paralyzing grief and depression.

You must decide whether you want to just *survive* CSA or *overcome* CSA, but if you continue to just survive, you won't experience the freedom you can receive from your spiritual heritage—God (The Holy Spirit, Christ). Just surviving CSA robs your life of the hope, joy, and peace that you can have. Through Christ's merciful, compassionate atonement, an Overcomer can envision the healed person they can become in Christ and work toward that goal. The past CSA may bring on exorbitant pain in your heart, but the hope of what can be in the future supersedes the deep despair of the isolation, guilt, humiliation, helplessness, worthlessness, and powerlessness of the past. And once you learn to manage CSA through an Overcomer approach, you are equipped to handle any future crises that life might hand you.

When you choose a new life as an Overcomer of CSA, you will look ahead for a hopeful present and future. You'll begin each day anew with Christ as your healer, rear guard, and leader. He will guide you each step of the way. You will work through and work out all the symptoms, fully undisturbed by ruminating thoughts about the CSA of the historic past.

Christ is an Overcomer's Redeemer, whether they've overcome CSA or any other crisis. He is the God of miraculous redemption. Through His immeasurable and ceaseless love, grace, and power, every child of God, no matter how victimized, shamed, weak, hopeless, or sinful, has an offer to be redeemed. An Overcomer's mantra is, *But one thing I do, forgetting those things which are behind and reaching forward to those things which are ahead, I press toward the goal for the prize of the upward call of God in Christ Jesus* (Philippians 3:13-14).

Christ always gives a victim a choice. The choice to choose Christ . . . or not. To choose to overcome . . . or not. Christ never forces Himself on any of His people. The free will God has given mankind is to be used on all decisions, including the decision to make Christ their Savior and Redeemer. Christian counselors just provide the treatment—Christ is the redemptive healer. Of course, it's not just victims who have this free will offer; it's everyone in this world . . . including sex offenders. Sadly, it's rare that a predator accepts Christ's offer for redemption. He might accept Him as Savior, yes, but truly repenting, accepting and living a redeemed life—no. This is because CSA offenders choose *not to* surrender their need for power and control and prefer the immediate sexual gratification (sin) they get from CSA instead of accepting God's powerful eternal redemption in their life.

Why do some victims not accept Christ's Overcomer redeemed life? The reasons are beyond the topic of this book, but they include allowing the consequences of the CSA trauma to rule over their life as opposed to choosing to believe in the living Christ and allowing Him to grant the abundant life He offers.

If you're having difficulty staying focused on overcoming the child sexual abuse you, your child, or both have endured, consider spending some extra alone time with the Lord. Some solitude with God will always calm you and others. Give Him time to renew your mind. Make an appointment with God to have a quiet time with Him daily; it will make a hundred-fold difference, because during that quiet time, the Holy Spirit will minister to you and guide you, just like God's Word promises He will.

Be kind to yourself—you have had to listen to and experience the details of your child's exploitation. Turn to God to process your secondary trauma pain. Yes, CSA is a beast, but Christ has already overcome the beast (devil)! He's already ever-present, just as He promises in His Word. He is holding your hand, walking you through the hurts of CSA: *For I, the LORD your God, will hold your right hand, Saying to you, "Fear not, I will help you"* (Isaiah 41:13).

He has offered to be your divine, loving Father in the midst of your joys and your sorrows—take the offer today! Receive God's mercy, consolation, comfort, strength, and guidance, because He fully understands your suffering, and He cares for you immensely. Step up to His throne of compassion and completely surrender your life and painful circumstances to Him in deep prayer and supplication. Then, receive the serene peace of mind which only He can provide. Give thanks to God and His Holy Spirit for guiding you through the labyrinth of child sexual abuse.

Thank Him for having strengthened you time after time in the past, and for giving you the words and actions today, telling you when to speak and when not to speak. Thank Him in advance for what He, as your Refuge and Shelter from CSA, is about to do for you, your child, and your future generations. In biblical times, Hebrew families would bless their children by laying their hands on them and praying over them as a sign of acceptance and anointment. Picture God laying His Hand upon your shoulder, His other Hand anointing your forehead, and giving you His acceptance—His blessing as a child of God. His child—going forward healed and healthy!

If your child has been molested or assaulted, you and he will need some time to grieve the loss of his respect and purity. But all the while, even through the grieving process, remain steadfast in giving glory to God, because our heavenly Father—the living God and our Redeemer has not left you to grieve alone. Thank Him that He is still in Command over the evil forces of the world. He alone has supreme heavenly authority over all the evil and grief on earth. As the most powerful One, He is also the King of grace. Ask for His mercy and grace!

The Lord is with you and your child as you watch him mourn the loss of his innocence. Matthew 5:4 promises that those who mourn will be comforted. Mourning can be about the loss of a loved one or anything that has been lost or stolen. When you seek and reach out to God, He is available to comfort both of you through His Holy Spirit. The Lord knows you and your child's sorrow and pain. Isaiah 66:13 says that as a mother comforts her child, God comforts us.

Soon, through God's support and comfort, you and your child will be able to return to your normal home routines, and He will restore your usual appropriate love and affection for one another. You and your child will let go of your fears about affection and closeness from others because you will have overcome CSA. Pray to Him. After quiet prayer times with God, an Overcomer goes forward with freshly renewed impetus!

God's Word calls us to be *still* in His presence. Being still—to praise God for His love and comfort, to listen to what He has to say, and to pray to Him and make your requests known to Him—requires a mindful structure and self-discipline on your behalf. But, as you become consistent in your pattern of having that daily quiet time with Him, you will look forward to it. You'll yearn to worship Him and grow in your relationship with Him. Make it a fun quiet-time journey. Plan on a favorite refreshment, snack, or meal while you sit in His Presence.

If you have never established a daily quiet time with God or have walked away from that daily commitment, the following is a guideline using the ACTS acronym—Adoration, Confession, Thanksgiving, and Supplication—to organize your daily personal time with Him:

1. First, be *still*. Come to Him in *Adoration* for His holiness and other attributes.Quiet and empty your mind blank of all thoughts other than confessing any sin that may interfere with your being in the holy presence of God (Psalm 46:10, 62:1,5).

2. Second, sing or play praise and worship songs (Psalm 100:2). *Confess* any sin against others and Him. Ask for His forgiveness and redemption. As you slow your mind from busy, racing thoughts, thank Him for His Presence, forgiveness, for your restoration of His relationship with you, for hearing you, and for answering. *It shall come to pass that before they call, I will answer; and while they are still speaking, I will hear* (Isaiah 65:24).

3. Third, *mindfully* pray to Him. Prayer is the intentional transfer of your praises, thoughts, and afflictions to God. You are encouraged to trust Him and to pour out your heart to Him because He *is* your refuge (Psalm 62:8). He has invited you to cast your cares upon Him and to transmit your burdens unto Him. Release all your anxieties to Him because *you are* His personal concern—He cares about you! (1 Peter 5:7, Matthew 11:28-30). And while releasing your burdens, *Thank* Him for what He has done and *will do* in your life and the lives of others.

4. Fourth, make your requests known to God through your *Supplications* (petitions/prayer requests). *Be anxious for nothing, but in everything by prayer and supplication, with thanksgiving, let your requests be made known to God* (Philippians 4:6).

A daily quiet time with God will refresh and renew your mind. As you read God's Word or use a devotional, workbook, or journal, remember that reading and spending time in His Word is the same as having Christ in your presence: *And the Word became flesh and dwelt among us, and we beheld His glory, the glory as of the only begotten of the Father, full of grace and truth* (John 1:14).

Plan to spend quality as well as quantity time with God. Although our society is designed to receive everything instantly, don't rush through God's Word and time in His Presence or you'll miss the opportunity to get to know Him. You'll miss the opportunity for Him to love on you, to speak to you, and to guide you.

Being still requires pausing and stopping there to rest in His Presence—in His peace. It is a state of releasing any fears and accepting the calmness of His Being. It is a process of transferring His peace over to your soul. He has offered you His peace: *Peace I leave with you, My peace I give to you; not as the world gives do I give to you. Let not your heart be troubled, neither let it be afraid* (John 14:27).

He freely gives His peace over to you. Take it. It's yours to be had. Not only during your quiet times, but all the time. Receive it! *Become complete. Be of good comfort, be of one mind, live in peace; and the God of love and peace will be with you* (2 Corinthians 13:11). Peace is doable, even in the midst of the dark adversity of this world. In view of the immoral, unsafe, corrupt, and dark world we live in, many folks believe that peace is just an ideal. However, peace remains from the beginning of time as one of God's greatest love offerings to us.

Peace is an eternal gift, and all who know God intimately can experience it daily simply by asking for it. This doesn't mean that those who have a personal relationship with God and who have His indescribable peace will escape the darkness of this world. It means they possess a valuable gift that's more powerful than the spirit of darkness. Christ's peace is not a passive dynamic that denies the truth about the dark world we live in. It's a peace that creates a world lit by His presence. It's a peace that gives us a positive, joyful outlook because of faith and trust in the God Who created the world.

Regardless of how ominous the present and future appear after a child has been molested or assaulted, every detail is still under God's power, *not* the sexual offender's. God still reigns as the God of justice over His creation, and He has not abandoned the child or his loved ones. Remember, God loves you, and He is gazing at you compassionately through His divine eyes. He *sees* your child, He sees you, and He sees whomever has inflicted pain upon you. Genesis 16:13 says that God is the God Who *sees* us. You and your child are the apple of His eye (Deuteronomy 32:10). God's justice is visible when He speaks protectively against anyone that attempts to harm his children, *for he who touches you touches the apple of His eye* (Zechariah 2:8).

Believing that God takes care of those who return His love and having faith that God will work out the healing process and turn what has happened through man's sinfulness into good (Romans 8:28) enables the child and those who care about him to maintain a mindfully healthy, well-balanced attitude of calmness and expectation. Expectation of what? The expectation of God's faithfulness to answer your prayers. The expectation that His help will come through! *God is our refuge and strength, a very present help in trouble, therefore we will not fear* (Psalm 46:1-2).

It is of utmost importance for an Overcomer to maintain the disposition of *expectation* because having expectation means having faith. Having an expectation is having an unwavering trust in God's providence. This leads to a confidence that one can manage the present and future with hope, courage, and serenity. God has always had an extraordinary and significant purpose and calling for you and your child, before and after abuse. Frankly, there are only two choices after a child has been molested or sexually assaulted: You can work out the past, present, and future *without* God's guidance and assistance and remain distraught, anxious, depressed, and fearful; or you can *believe* and *accept* that God is faithful in His Word when He promises His Presence, His Help, and His Spirit of comfort and guidance.

But the Helper, the Holy Spirit, whom the Father will send in My name, He will teach you all things, and bring to your remembrance all things that I said to you (John 14:26).

You can believe in His justice . . . or not.

For the LORD is a God of justice (Isaiah 30:18).

You can acknowledge His vengeance . . . or not.

"Vengeance is Mine, I will repay," says the Lord (Romans 12:19).

You can face the past, present, and future after sexual abuse with *trust, hope,* and *confidence* . . . or you can not.

God created His people for fellowship with Him. He wants you to turn to Him whenever you are in a crisis, but it is ultimately your choice to include Him. Some parents and caregivers not only experience fear during their CSA circumstances, but they add to their concerns a *fear of God*. God does not have to be feared. He is a God of love and grace. If fear is to be overcome amidst the trauma of CSA, it is vital that the parent or caregiver seek God to be one in spirit with Him so that the Holy Spirit can work in and through them. Having God work through the process of CSA prevention and protection helps you to face any challenges or danger encountered—with God's divine intervention. A child sexual abuse crisis can wear out a parent's/caregiver's coping reserves. God's intervention provides strength and hope. His intervention sends an upsurge of the Holy Spirit, which overflows in the hearts of those who call on Him.

Remember some pages back we discussed the objective of creating an Overcomer environment (home) for your child? The *trust, hope,* and *confidence* within you are fueled through the same promise Christ made in John 16:33, when He said, *These things I have spoken to you, that in Me you may have peace. In the world you will have tribulation; but be of good cheer, I have overcome the world.* Do you believe that promise? Christ has offered that you can be of good *cheer* (joy) and live in *peace*, because even if you go through tribulations like CSA, HE has overcome them all! Christ has *overcome* the world. He *is* an Overcomer!

God says that He created mankind in His Image (Genesis 1:27). So you and all of your loved ones are copies of Him. Can you rejoice because of what God and His Son have said? God created you to be *like Him*, and His Son has overcome the world. That makes His Son *and you* Overcomers!

What is required of you to become an Overcomer? Faith in Christ—that is all. 1 John 5:4 says *whatever is born of God overcomes the world. And this is the victory that has overcome the world—our faith.* You can live your life fully and abundantly as an Overcomer (in spite of CSA). CSA will not overcome you—*you* will overcome CSA.

If you open a thesaurus, or search one online, you will find a long list of synonyms for overcome. Gather up *all* your divine mighty energy right now, go to a thesaurus, and pick a word or words that are synonymous with the word *overcome*. So which word(s) did you pick? Which of these words are you going to use to *overcome* child sexual abuse?

It's important to note that it's not that an Overcomer should live so deeply in the realm of heavenly holy ground that he or she is unable to be of any value to those in the world who have no connection with Christ. Instead, an Overcomer needs that divine connection with Christ in order to be of value to his or her children and to *everyone*. An Overcomer refrains from focusing on CSA pain by asking God to protect his/her mind and his/her children's minds from sad and hurtful thoughts. These thoughts only serve to bring down the spirit, destroy and prevent good relationships, and block progress toward encouragement, peace, and His joy.

When past or present thoughts of discouragement take over, there's no positive future to be had. Hide Proverbs 4:23 in your heart as a reminder to be diligent about your thoughts, because this verse says that your thoughts become the *issues* of your life. Overcomers choose to be nourished and fortified by His healing love, thoughts, and unsurpassable power through the darkness of CSA. Those are God's instructions for how He wants you and your child to live. This approach makes the dark side of life hopeful and makes life in this world worth living. When an Overcomer approach is used to address and treat CSA, the recovered and healed child is the handiwork of God: *For we are His workmanship, created in Christ Jesus for good works, which God prepared beforehand that we should walk in them* (Ephesians 2:10).

When times get overwhelming, the soundlessness of silence is good. It is enjoyed and appreciated as a gift from God. *Being still in silence* brings the reflective awareness that we are alone with God. The Spirit, Mind, and Body welcome the restoration of relaxing quiet. The soundlessness of silence is especially restorative and healing when our spirit is receptive to listen for God's presence, which is powerfully felt and heard during those quiet alone moments with Him. It is in that silence that we sense and feel His *living* presence and Holy Spirit's divine Being within, renewing our spirit with astounding and inspirational empowerment.

The only time silence is not good, however, is when child sexual abuse is involved. Speaking up and speaking out is good. Taking action so that something is *done* to resolve the problem is good. If you sit still and do nothing, child sexual abuse becomes like a fire that cannot be put out. The only stillness that's good when the fire of CSA burns is being still to know that He is God (Psalm 46:10) and to listen for His still small voice. Otherwise, it's like sitting in a dark abyss that's spiraling downward—it leaves a deep, dark hole in your heart.

CSA can only be overcome if you listen to that gentle whisper telling you to be proactive. It's telling you that when there's a CSA fire, let out the silent secret and tell! The sound of your telling then brings on prevention, protection, and healing!

> *And after the earthquake a fire, but the LORD was not in the fire; and after the fire a still small voice* (1 Kings 19:12).

> *To Him who rides on the heaven of heavens, which were of old! Indeed, He sends out His voice, a mighty voice* (Psalm 68:33).

When a CSA Overcomer listens for God's *mighty voice,* it is then and only then that God's voice of *peace* and *power* over CSA can be heard. The road to recovery without God's help is a lifelong upward climb that leads nowhere.

This book has discussed numerous *high-risk factors* for CSA. Being aware of these high-risk factors and the long-term consequences of CSA helps us understand the most mindful and productive pathways to take in order to resolve the problem of child sexual abuse. But these high-risk factors are not the sole cause of CSA. And knowing these factors is not a sole method of prevention. The fact is, there is darkness in the world. The sexual abuse of children does not come from the light of God. It involves the devil's darkness and his minions, and the evil that is in his agenda for the world. The devil *is* a high-risk factor. The Bible instructs us to be watchful because the devil prowls around, seeking to devour us (1 Peter 5:8).

In Job 1:7, Christ asks the devil where he has just come from. The devil answers that he has come from going to and fro on the earth, walking back and forth on it. The devil wants to keep the darkness of child sexual abuse as his little secret. He wants the people on earth to be silent about CSA. He doesn't want us telling. He wants to keep it a secret so that he can invite more children into the silence of abuse. He wants to have those children become grownups within the trauma and darkness of CSA.

The Bible warns us in 2 Corinthians 11:14 that the devil disguises himself as an angel of light. What does that tell us? It tells us that we, as adults, and our children need to be *aware* and *mindful* of humans who disguise themselves as good people but have the devil's darkness within them. But the good news is that the Bible says the reason the Son of God (Christ) appeared on earth was to destroy the works of the devil (1 John 3:8). Christ said that he came to earth so that we could have and live our lives fully and abundantly. The opposite is true of the devil—he is here to steal, kill, and destroy our lives (John 10:10).

We are encouraged that we can outwit the devil by becoming aware and not being ignorant to his schemes and manipulation. We don't have to be caught off guard by his efforts to tempt us into sin (2 Corinthians 2:11). We are also reminded that if we submit our lives to God and resist the devil, the devil will flee from us (James 4:7).

The devil's role on earth has always been to sow seeds of doubt, fear, anxiety, confusion, discouragement, and hopelessness. It is when a victim of CSA (or other abuse) is most vulnerable that the devil likes to show up. The devil is a deceiver who loves confusion in a victim's life to further complicate the crisis. Do not let the devil's shrewdness and manipulative whispers of despair overpower God's mighty voice!

Have you ever heard God's mighty voice? God's voice is calling to free you and your child from the trauma of child sexual abuse. True freedom comes with responsibility—are you being a responsible parent or caregiver? If you are, you will experience the freedom of peace of mind. Freedom from the trauma of CSA or any other trauma can only be experienced if your human spirit is willing to surrender living in the past with CSA in exchange for loving and serving God.

Many victims live in slavery to the past. They live in slavery to CSA. But they may not even realize they're enslaved because they have normalized their symptoms and have grown so accustomed to them, they don't realize it. The symptoms and the pain have become the habits of their life. Yes, depression, anxiety, fear, eating disorders, and other symptoms can become habits. These habits are reflected in the victim's daily living. Their CSA trauma, which they've accepted as a part of life, reveals their slavery. And their slavery keeps them from being free.

The Bible presents God's plan to bring freedom to the captives—to all of His people who are oppressed by destructive, evil forces: *The Spirit of the LORD is upon Me, because He has anointed Me to preach the gospel to the poor; He has sent Me to heal the brokenhearted, to proclaim liberty to the captives and recovery of sight to the blind, to set at liberty those who are oppressed* (Luke 4:18). Christ is offered as the solution—instead of living a life of sin or allowing others' sin to permeate in one's life.

The plan is for Christ's forgiveness to free all His people and for them to be unshackled from the devil's evil forces. That is the gift of freedom Christ offers. But it must be accepted in faith and responsibility. If you decide to accept God's gift of freedom, you will be transformed into a new free being who will experience deliverance from CSA symptoms and will step into a new love and veritable peace with Christ and all of those around you.

Many may scoff at your decision to turn toward Christ to guide your life. However, those scoffers can't offer you a life of stability. They can only offer their weakness and human thinking. Looking to Christ for everything that you undertake becomes one of the most important decisions you will make in your life. Christ offers, through the power of the Holy Spirit, what the scoffers cannot—and that is the security of knowing what is best for you, your child, and your family at any given moment.

When and if you accept God's plan, will, and purpose for your life, you will become ever so aware of the shortcomings and fallibility of humanity and the short-term aspects of this world. God's holy plan for you and your child will unfold as you make Him your go-to for everything in your life!

In Ephesians 4:21-24, Paul talks about the damage that can result from misconduct. He knew that antisocial or immoral behaviors (sin) only lead to more sin, and that they contribute to a destructive relationship with others and a separation from God. Paul considered the inappropriate behaviors he outlined as remnants of the "former conduct" and the "old man"—who we are before Christ. Paul teaches that when a person puts on the "new man," the spirit of his mind is renewed. He urges that when the spirit of the mind is renewed, a person is then able to yield to Christ and the Holy Spirit's influence in their life. He submits that it is with that renewed mind that a person has the ability to control his conduct.

A parent or caregiver of a child who has been subjected to CSA must examine the self for any amount of the old, unhealthy, non-renewed mind. Not having mindfully renewed the mind can result in former conduct (words/actions) overruling the work toward establishing an Overcomer home for your child and family. The person with a renewed mind is known for their *awareness* of CSA or any other abuse. They are known for being caring, for calmness, for tenderness, and respect for the needs of the child and others. The goal of the renewed mind is to build up the relationship with Christ, the child, and others, rather than to destroy relationships.

> *If indeed you have heard Him and have been taught by Him, as the truth is in Jesus: that you put off, concerning your former conduct, the old man which grows corrupt according t o the deceitful lusts, and be renewed in the spirit of your mind, and that you put on the new man which was created according to God, in true righteousness and holiness* (Ephesians 4:21-24).

Whether or not there is a sexual abuse problem, the question remains. Have you submitted your life to God (Christ)? Has your child submitted his life to God? Has your family submitted their lives to God? If you have not submitted your life to God and accepted Christ as your personal Savior, or if you need to return into a personal relationship with Him, today is a good day to pray and ask Him to come into your life. Pray with me:

> *God of mercy and grace, I surrender and offer my life to You because I believe that Your Son died for my sins and the sins of the world, to forgive us for our sins*

against You. I believe You are the God Who created the world, and I now ask for your forgiveness for the sins I've committed against Your Will. Give me the strength to start anew, with You as the center of my life. Your Word promises that when we ask for it, Your power of protection will be over our lives and over our children's lives. I claim that power of safety over child sexual abuse for my children. Make my child invisible to perpetrators. Whisper in my ear and in my child's ear when we need to be alert and use our body safety plan. Keep my child's growing mind and body safe. Create laws that will empower families to move away from and stop CSA. Father, grow me in my life with You now to do Your Will. Don't let my commitment to You or my children fade into complacency. In Your Redeeming Name, Amen.

The daily child-rearing decisions and choices you make could have far-reaching consequences for both you and your child, spiritually, emotionally, and physically. Resolve today to strengthen the prevention and protection boundaries your child needs in order for him to experience body safety for life. This is God's will—that your child feels loved and safe at home and in the world around him!

ENDNOTES

1   Snyder, H.N. (2000). *Sexual Assault of Young Children as Reported to Law Enforcement: Victim, Incident, and Offender Characteristics.* Washington, DC: U.S. Department of Justice.

2   Ibid

3   Becker, J.V. & Hunter, J.A. (1997). Understanding and treating child and adolescent sexual offenders. In T.H. Ollendick & R.J. Prinz (Eds.), *Advances in Clinical Child Psychology, 19.* New York: Plenum Press.

4   U.S. Department of Justice, Bureau of Justice Statistics. (2006). *Percent of victimizations reported to the police, by type of crime and age of victims.* http://www.ojp.usdoj.gov/bjs/pub/pdf/cvus/current/cv0696.pdf.

5   Whitman, B. (2002). Psychological and psychitaric issues. In A.P Giardino & E.R. Giardino (Eds.), *Recognition of Child Abuse by the Mandated Reporter, Third Edition.* St. Louis: G.W. Medical Publishing.

6   Ibid.

7   Anda, F.R., Chapman, D.P., Croft, J.B., Dietz, P.M., Felitti, V.J., Marks, J.S., et al. (2001). Abused boys, battered mothers, and male involvement in teen pregnancy. *Pediatrics, 107*(2), E19.

8   Leslie, M.B., Nyamathi, A., & Stein, J.A. (2002). Relative contributions of parent substance abuse and childhood maltreatment to chronic homelessness, depression, and substance abuse problems among homeless women: Mediating roles of self-esteem and abuse in adulthood. *Child Abuse and Neglect, 26* (10), 1011-1027.

9   Anda, R.F., Brown, D.W., Dong, M., Dube, S.R., Felitti, V.J., Giles, W.H., et al. (2005). Long-term consequences of childhood sexual abuse by gender of victim. *American Journal of Preventive Medicine, 28* (5), 430-438.

RESOURCES

Childhelp USA
National Child Abuse Hotline: 1.800.4.A.CHILD (1.800.422.4453)
All calls are confidential and anonymous.
www.childhelpusa.org
Provides information, literature, programs directly serving abused children and their families. Provides local telephone numbers to report abuse or access crisis intervention, and referrals to emergency, social service, and support resources.

The Safer Society Foundation
P.O. Box 340
Brandon, VT 05733-0340
Office: 802.247.3132 Fax: 802.247.4233 *Call for a referral to a local CSA treatment provider for a child, adolescent, or adult.* (M-F, 9–4:30 p.m. ET).
www.safersociety.org

Child Molestation Research and Prevention Institute
P.O. Box 7593
Atlanta, GA 30357
Office: 404.872.5152
www.childmolestationprevention.org
Online directory for CSA therapists for evaluation and treatment.

National Advocacy Center (NCAC)
210 Pratt Ave NE
Huntsville, AL 35801
Call to receive referral to your local Child Advocacy Center
256-533-KIDS (5437)
Provides training, prevention, and treatment services for child abuse and neglect.
Mission: Providing each child who has suffered abuse with justice, hope, and healing.

National Center on Sexual Behavior of Youth
940 N.E. 13th St., 3B-3406
Oklahoma City, OK 73104
Office: 405.271.8858
www.ncsby.org
Information concerning sexual development and youth sexual behavior concerns.

National Center for Victims of Crime (NCVC)
2000 M St., NW, Suite 480
Washington, DC 20036
Office: 202.467.8700 Fax: 202.467.8701
Toll-free: 1.800.FYI.CALL (1.800.394.2255)
TDD: 1.800.211.7996
Email: webmaster@ncvc.org or gethelp@ncvc.org
www.ncvc.org
CSA victim information and referral center. Database has over 30,000 organizations. Refers callers for crisis intervention, counseling, support groups, research information, assistance with the criminal justice process, and referrals to local attorneys.

National Center for Missing & Exploited Children®
333 John Carlyle Street, Suite #125
Alexandria, Virginia 22314-5950
Has a CSA online library.
To report information about a missing child:
24-hour call center: **1-800-THE-LOST (1-800-843-5678)**
Phone: 703-224-2150 Fax: 703-224-2122
To report child sexual exploitation use the CyberTipline®.

Safe4Athletes
P.O. Box 650
Santa Monica, CA 90406
1-855-723-3422
www.safe4athletes.org/
info@safe4athletes.org
Mission: Advocate for athlete welfare where every athlete is provided a safe and positive environment free of abuse, bullying and harassment.

Stop It Now!®
Office: 413.587.3500
Helpline: 1.888.PREVENT (1.888.773.8368)
Email: helpline@stopitnow.org
Website: www.stopitnow.org

DARKNESS to LIGHT
1064 Gardner Road, Suite 210
Charleston, SC 29407
24/7 TOLL FREE CONFIDENTIAL CALLING
Trained Crisis Counselor, Support and Resources.
National Helpline: 866.FOR.LIGHT
Office: 843.965.5444 Fax: 843-571-0902
https://www.d2l.org/get-help/national-resources

Darkness to Light
Offers training that specializes in the education and prevention of child sexual abuse, other forms of abuse, and mandated reporting. Stewards of Children®, the flagship program, teaches adults how to prevent, recognize, and react responsibly to child sexual abuse.
Product and Training Information & General Product Information
Stewards@D2L.org

Stewards of Children® Prevention Toolkit
The *Stewards of Children®* Prevention Toolkit Mobile App can be downloaded for parents and caregivers to learn about how to protect their children from sexual abuse.

Protect Young Eyes: Defending Kids from Online Danger
"How to Block Porn on Any Device for Free" by Chris McKenna
https://protectyoungeyes.com

World Childhood Foundation Inc.
900 3rd Ave. 29th Floor
New York, NY 10022
212-867-6088
Website: info@childhood-USA.org
Mission: To stimulate, promote and enable the development of solutions to prevent and address sexual abuse, exploitation and violence against children.

ANOTHER WESTBOW PRESS BOOK
BY REINA DAVISON

Overcoming Abuse: My Body Belongs to God and Me This book provides examples of proper and improper affection and the difference between good touch (God touch) and no touch! The child is taught how to identify a no touch person. Body safety is taught for protection at home, in the community, and on the internet. When your child is taught that he can overcome any troubles, that his body was created by God and that it is an amazing gift from Him, he allows God and himself the ownership of his body. This ownership empowers your child to say "NO!" when a person approaches him with improper affection; it liberates him to tell a trusted adult when he feels scared and unsafe. This book will help your child to use his mind in order for him to live as God intended—loved and safe.

To bring the message of *Overcoming Abuse: My Body Belongs to God and Me* to your organization, church, or event, visit: **www.overcomingabuse.info**

ABOUT THE BOOK

Sexual abuse is a challenging topic for most parents to discuss, especially with their children. But, as unpleasant as the subject may be, sexual abuse is an essential conversation for all parents and caregivers to have with their children; it's a serious, heart-rending, everyday problem in the world that affects both male and female children. In *Overcoming Abuse: Child Sexual Abuse Prevention and Protection*, author Reina Davison offers an encyclopedic manual for parents, caregivers or helpers to educate their self and train children on body safety. Davison presents a reservoir of information on the dynamics of child sexual abuse, the sex offender profile, and how to protect and prevent a child from being a target of child sexual abuse anywhere, including the internet. This extensive resource instructs the adult on initiating conversation to help the child gain an understanding about the precious gift of his body. It introduces and walks the adult through a healthy, age-appropriate biblical perspective on human sexuality. *Overcoming Abuse: Child Sexual Abuse Prevention and Protection* spells out the process of preventing and overcoming child sexual abuse and offers hope and healing. It helps parents, caregivers, and all adults to reassure children that home is where love is, and child sexual abuse is not.